Thoughts to Hear With Your Heart

On Jewish Inspiration and Life

Sarah Karmely

DWELLING PLACE
PUBLICATIONS

Published by:
Dwelling Place Publications
1651 President Street
Brooklyn, N.Y. 11213
www.DwellingPublications.com

Questions to the author may be sent to sarah@sarahkarmely.org.
For booking information, please contact info@sarahkarmely.org.
To keep up-to-date with the author's latest happenings, please
visit www.SarahKarmely.org.

Permissions:
"Changing the Jewish World," from the *N'shei Chabad Newsletter*:
Flagship Lubavitch women's magazine, Rishe Deitsch, editor;
Subscription info: 718-756-8492.

Design by Devorah Haggar Graphic Design

Printed in Canada

ISBN-13: 978-0-9799172-0-2 paperback
ISBN-10: 0-9799172-0-4 paperback

About the Cover:

The significance of the imagery of two lameds face-to-face —
The Jewish Heart — was made public and explained by the one of
the greatest medieval Kabbalists, Rabbi Abraham Abulafia. The
depiction here was painted by Michoel Muchnik of **MuchnikArts.com**.
For more about this mystical symbol, and to purchase Jewelry based on
Rabbi Abulafia's teachings, please visit **www.inner.org/goldjewelry**

Acknowledgments

I must first thank G-d for giving me so much: my Rebbe, my spiritual life, and the *koach* (power) to touch so many people with my life. Thank you, Hashem, for everything.

A special thank you goes first to Rabbi Moshe Lazar, among the Lubavitcher Rebbe's *shluchim* (representatives) to Milan, Italy. As the head of that city's Persian youth synagogue and my introduction to Chabad, Rabbi Lazar suggested once that I write a book. "Really?" I asked, surprised. "Yes! Just take all your *N'shei Chabad Newsletter* columns and put them in book form." Without you, Rabbi Lazar, there'd be no book. Thank you so much.

My Italian connection doesn't end there. I deeply thank Rabbi Lazar's wonderful wife Judy for her love and support. The Garelik family of Milan, the head *shluchim* there, played an important role in my life. I studied regularly with Mrs. Bassie Garelik, and I would like to single her out for acknowledgement as I acknowledge her beautiful family. Acknowledgement goes as well to Rabbi Shmuel Rodal, another Chabad *shliach* (representative) and my children's teacher in Milan.

The wonderful people who stop me in the street to tell me they liked my articles that they read in the *N'shei Chabad Newsletter* have a special place in my heart. Thank you all for giving me the encouragement and impetus to carry on, and for reminding me that words do have power. I likewise thank all the *shluchim* who tell me they use my articles in their speeches.

A special acknowledgment goes to my copy editor, Rishe Deitsch, the sage, sensitive editor of the distinguished *N'shei Chabad Newsletter,* for always being there for me. Rishe helped me in so many ways. Besides editing my articles, which at times needed significant improvement, she continues to guide me gently, helping me, and encouraging me to write more articles. I thank her for giving me a forum, and I thank her for critically contributing to the book's editing.

A special thank you to Mrs. Rivkie Geisinsky, editor-in-chief of the *N'shei Chabad Newsletter,* for playing an important part in bringing my writing and experiences to the light of print, and to her wonderful son, Yehudah Leib Geisinsky, for painstakingly making copies of all my articles from the archives.

For the final construction of the book you have before you, admiration is due to Rabbis Mendy Hecht and Zalman Nelson for their skillful editing of the text; Mrs. Bracha Sternfield for her careful proofreading expertise; and Yonason Gordon of Dwelling Place Publications for his proficiency in overseeing the book's production.

I acknowledge the hardworking Rabbi Moshe Rubashkin, a community activist of distinction, and his *aishet chayil* (praiseworthy wife) Faiga, for their most honorable help, and I thank Mrs. Chaya Sara Zarchi for her moral support and constant encouragement.

The one and only Rabbi Manis Friedman, dean of the legendary Bais Chana women's school in Minneapolis, Minnesota and my *mashpiah* (spiritual mentor), a guide in my life, deserves special praise. Much of my thinking comes from the probing answers he provided to my toughest questions. Of course, thanks also go to the rabbi's wife, Rebbetzin Chanie Friedman, for all her support. Thank you so much, Rabbi and Mrs. Friedman.

I thank my beloved children: David Yecheskel and wife Chana Devorah (née Koenigsberg); daughter Shoshana Esther and husband Mordechai Rofeh; daughter Daniella Miriam and husband Elroyi Binyamin Gemal; and my dear grandchildren who bring so much love into my life.

At this point, I must especially acknowledge the brave heart and soul of my beloved son David. More than any other of my articles, the ones telling his poignant true story of heartbreak and hope continue to draw hot tears from readers as they are touched by tenderness and triumph. Thank you, David, for allowing others to take inspiration from you and benefit from your message.

Thank you to my entire dear family, brothers, sisters, brothers-in-law and sisters-in-law, and my faithful friends for the moral support they have always given me. And among my friends, I don't know how to express my gratitude and fondness for Odette and Jimmy Fellus, whose graciousness and kindness to me and my family is beyond words — not only to us, but to all the many lives whom they touch.

Words will never be enough, but I now make a special acknowledgement to my husband Benjamin, for always being there for me — your patience and support help me, and you both encourage me and challenge me to continue when I feel I cannot anymore.

Finally, how do you say thank you to our Rebbe? (How can anyone say thank you to any Rebbe for what he does for us? Words aren't enough!) The Rebbe's the one who set me on my feet — and then he gave me wings! Without the Rebbe, I wouldn't be where I am right now. And I would certainly not be writing this book. He gave me my life. Thank you, Rebbe. Thank you will never be good enough ... but it's the least I can say.

Sarah Karmely
11 Cheshvan, 5768
October 23, 2007

Table of Contents

Foreword

A good relationship with one's parents provides a sense of security. A good relationship with one's teacher promotes confidence in one's abilities. A good relationship with one's spouse cultivates a sense of belonging; with co-workers, a sense of accomplishment; with children, a sense of fulfillment. Sarah Karmely, has a relationship with the Lubavitcher Rebbe, of blessed memory. Not only does this supply her with all the above mentioned benefits, it also engenders a sense of mission — a transcendent mission.

She found in the Rebbe a model of selfless commitment to changing the world — one person at a time, all the time. The Rebbe's passion became her passion and the Rebbe called her "my partner" in his holy work.

The moving chapters and stories of her book describe moments when she experienced a sense of fulfillment, feelings of accomplishment, security and confidence. She also describes a sense of belonging. But a true student acquires something of the teacher's style, something of his power. As such, Mrs. Karmely represents the Rebbe's style with the greatest fealty; her intuition is an unerring reflection to her listeners and readers of something of the Rebbe himself.

Whenever she addresses groups or counsels individuals her words are effective, her enthusiasm infectious, her commitment compelling, and through her many who never knew the Rebbe feel a connection as though they too were touched by the Rebbe.

As you read, you may find yourself growing envious of the connection to the Rebbe and admiring her commitment to the holy work of Tikun Olam, improving the world one person at a time, all the time.

If her example moves us to devote at least some part of our day or week to our generation's mission of world betterment, as described by the Rebbe; if we ask ourselves, "What have I done to make the world better"; if we go to the Rebbe's Ohel (grave site) and commit ourselves to his teachings and works; that would be Mrs. Karmely's reward, her success. If we become better people, it would also be the Rebbe's reward and success. After all, they are 'partners', are they not?

Rabbi Manis Friedman

Prolouge

In listening to people's stories, one thing has become clear to me: no story ever begins. Wherever you start telling the story, it is preceded by people, events and situations that set the scene for the following events. As such, unless the reader is privy to some of the background, the present tale – whatever it is – will have little meaning. To say it more simply, regardless of where you decide to start your story, your listeners will, to some degree, be joining the action right in the middle.

Taking that idea to the logical extreme by considering our parents' stories and their parents' stories, it becomes clear that all stories begin with Adam and Eve – our foremost parents – and ultimately with G-d, Creator of the Universe. In essence, all of our stories begin with G-d whether we are aware of it or not.

The Baal Shem Tov, the illustrious founder of the Chassidic movement, used stories to teach profound and catalyzing lessons about G-d. And, my own story clearly started with G-d; although, I assure you, it is something I only now realize. I was oblivious at the time.

I trace my ancestry to a family of Jews from Mashhad, Iran, but I grew up in Stamford Hill, London, very near to the heart of Orthodox Jewry in England. Our family was traditional. We kept strictly kosher, lit candles on Shabbat and my father wore a hat and a yarmulke, but life was somewhat superficial —

routinized behaviors that lacked a true feeling of joy, pleasure and a personal connection. Only now, in hindsight, do I realize that it was missing because I've experienced the power of Chassidic teachings to produce inspired and passionate action.

In 1965 I turned eighteen and married Benjamin Karmely. We moved to Milan, Italy, where I quickly had three children and settled into a rather normal, culturally modern yet traditional Jewish life. For thirteen years, I had everything any woman could want — A loving husband who supported us very nicely; three healthy children who were the light of my life; a lovely home, friends, good health … everything.

But all along, my whole life, something was missing. Ask me then and I couldn't have told you what it was. It was there, however, I knew it was there. It felt like a hollow core within that I incessantly tried to fill with countless "as-soon-as" thoughts like, "As soon as I finish school, everything will be perfect." And then, "As soon as I get married I will feel complete." And then, "As soon as we have children, everything will really be perfect." Nevertheless, there I was with everything and yet still something was missing.

Then, as now, Benjamin traveled a good deal for his business. One day I picked him up from the airport after a trip to Thailand. Even from a distance I could see that something was wrong. He was limping; he looked ill, pale and drawn and was obviously in pain. Although he insisted he was fine, he couldn't fool me.

Something was very wrong.

By the next morning there was no question. He awoke in excruciating pain and his whole body was in a state of spasm. He couldn't walk or move his legs, and even his speech was affected. We ran to the doctor and Benjamin was immediately hospitalized, despite the glaring fact that no one knew what exactly was wrong. Over the next several days he underwent test after test, but nothing proved conclusive. All the while he was getting worse and worse. At times he was partially paralyzed; constantly he was in serious pain. He couldn't even get out of bed. Several times a day I went to the hospital to bring him kosher food, which we regularly ate. It seemed especially important at that point, yet hope faded as I watched his continued deterioration. The days turned into weeks. I started losing hope when the painful bone marrow tests failed to indicate a cause. The worst day came about a month after he was originally hospitalized. Arriving at the hospital slightly earlier than usual, I came upon my usually stoic husband collapsed in tears.

Seeing him so distraught obliterated the remnant of my own defenses. I marched over to the doctors, convinced they were concealing information, and demanded they tell me what was wrong. "We don't know," they insisted. "We have no idea what it could be." And, since they didn't know the cause, they had no clear indication of what treatment to begin. "We need more tests," they said over and over again. "How long will this go on?" I numbly asked. The doctors shrugged. "We don't know. Maybe in a few months things will improve."

Months? I was stunned by the bleak prognosis. No, it was more than that — I was depressed, I was frustrated and I felt totally lost. My husband was our strong protector who always knew what to do. But with him so very ill I felt alone and frightened. I didn't know what to do, or where to turn. I returned home from the hospital that day exhausted. My phone was ringing as I walked in the door.

It was my usual weekly call from Rabbi Moshe Lazar, a Chabad rabbi in Milan who had become a good friend. "How is your husband?" he wanted to know. I couldn't answer. All I could do was cry.

Then it came out of nowhere, like a lone ray of sunshine piercing a thick dark rain cloud. Rabbi Lazar held out a straw of hope I hadn't thought of before. "Why don't you ask for a blessing from the Rebbe?" he asked. "The Rebbe" was the renowned Lubavitcher Rebbe, Rabbi Menachem Mendel Schneerson, from the Crown Heights section of Brooklyn, New York. I had never met the Rebbe, but I had heard stories. Everyone had. The Rebbe was said to be a holy, G-dly man capable of doing otherworldly things. "Why not," I thought. By this point, I was desperate, and besides, it couldn't hurt.

I gave Rabbi Lazar my husband's name and his mother's name so the proper blessing could be said, and he said he would call New York that very night. I thanked him, and we hung up.

I was grateful for the help. Having thought my options where completely exhausted, I felt a small sense of peace from doing something, anything. Honestly, I can't say that I hung up the phone brimming with confidence that we would be the beneficiaries of some kind of miracle. But deep down inside me was a small spark which I clutched tightly.

The next morning, looking for some company and moral support for a day I expected to be exhausting, I invited my father-in-law to come with me to the hospital. As we walked in, I remembered the blessing Rabbi Lazar said he would request, but decided against mentioning it to my father-in-law. No point in both of us being disappointed. We stepped out of the elevator on the third floor and I gazed down the hall toward the door of my husband's room.

Can you imagine our shock when we saw my formerly paralyzed husband *walking* toward us, *without crutches?*

Again, all I could do was cry — in fact, we all did. As well as I was able, between the sobs, I told the story of last night's call from Rabbi Lazar and the request for a blessing from the Lubavitcher Rebbe. And now … look!

There was, of course, no medical explanation from the doctors as to what the problem had been, or what had cured it. They simply didn't know. And neither was there ever a clear explanation, in my mind, for all the whys I had accumulated. Why us? Why my husband? Why was he chosen for the affliction — and then for the miracle cure?

"We don't presume to know the answers to those questions.

G-d has His plan," Rabbi Lazar said. "But," he reminded us, "there is one thing we do know: everything that happens to us is for the good. G-d uses His own means and devices – including afflictions, healings, or not healing – for our own good."

My husband had already come to that conclusion. When he returned home, he told me about the hospital days and nights he spent in pain, unable to walk, uncertain of his future. "I learned one thing for sure," he said. "There's more to life than just business and pleasure."

It was certainly true. And, quite obviously, everything did work out "for the best." But neither of us then, at that moment, knew the full impact of Benjamin's illness and recovery. G-d still had more plans for us.

This is the story of my beginning. It is the tale of how my association began with the Rebbe, with Chabad, and – in a new and different way – with G-d. He had always been there, of course. But this was the point, way back then in 1977, at which I chose to walk with Him.

This book is a journal of my spiritual adventure since that remarkable healing, complete with the stories I've been privileged to hear and in which I participated. I invite you to come along for the ride, and walk with Him too.

On Marriage

My Rebbe, The Peacemaker

After experiencing the blessing of my husband's cure, it would be nice to be able to write that from then on everything worked out perfectly: that my husband and I went on to live lives of joy, fulfillment and spiritual growth; that both of us assumed a more religiously observant lifestyle with ease and confidence; and that we rode off into the sunset amidst peaceful days.

But the world G-d fashioned is not some scripted movie, and that's not the way things usually work. Everyone experiences some problems, conflicts, pain and disappointment. It is misguided to think otherwise. However, it is also a mistake to think that you are the only one who struggles. All of us are challenged, over and over, whether or not it's seen. In fact, it is said that though our tests and challenges are difficult, they are an expression of G-d's affection and care in that they help us grow and achieve. Consider a parent who disciplines his child for the child's ultimate benefit, despite the short-term discomfort — for both of them.

In any event, our incredible experience of sickness and cure was quickly followed by a very serious spiritual test, one that could have had permanent and disastrous effects. Today, I know that every obstacle we face in life elevates us. But then, Benjamin and I hardly had time to bask in the glow of a new relationship with G-d when trouble arose.

What was the problem? A common one, actually. Married people, when they are spiritually inspired and start observing more Jewish law and custom, frequently encounter tension if they don't progress at the same pace. One spouse may be entirely ready, by noon on Tuesday, to accept all of the mitzvahs, with all of their ramifications, without further consideration. The other spouse might need a little more time — sometimes months or even years to think, to plan, to recognize and understand each step forward, to digest the mitzvahs in small bites.

The disparity in spiritual progress is hardly unpredictable. No two people ever grow at exactly the same pace in almost anything. Imagine a couple who enjoy taking a casual walk together for relaxation and pleasure. Consider the tension that would arise if one spouse became enamored of taking that "pleasurable" walk behind a little white golf ball while the other enjoyed it only occasionally; imagine the conflict. Their leisure time would likely be reorganized around tee times; their social life and choice of friends would change; work, religion, school and children's activities might be disrupted by the need to play.

But taking up golf is a minor disruption compared to the one my husband and I were about to face as we came to terms with the vast implications of my husband's illness and cure.

No question about it, the experience had set us both on a new path. We were inspired by the miracle and its revelation of something beyond the natural, logical order. G-d, spirituality and religion permeated our conversations, and together we set out to become more observant. One thing became clear to me: becoming an observant Jew is a highly addictive activity. The Torah tells us the reward for performing a mitzvah is another mitzvah — the more you fulfill, the more you want to fulfill. And, in terms of living a Jewish life, there is literally no end to the opportunities to perform more and more mitzvahs. An observant Jew's lifestyle imbues every day with spiritual significance. Not only is the daily schedule punctuated with prayer and worship morning, afternoon, night and at bedtime, but every other act – eating, dressing, bathing, grooming, use of leisure time, sleeping arrangements and even intimacy – is subject to an all-encompassing set of Jewish laws that mandate when, how and under what conditions everyday activities are to be accomplished.

Back to our couple. What happens if one spouse is not ready to move into full observance as quickly as the other? What if one feels, "I'm ready right now," while the other is thinking, "Can't we just take it a little slower?" It is complicated when the wife progresses more quickly than her husband, and even more so when it is the husband who progresses more quickly. Take celebrating the myriad of Jewish holidays, for example. It's a huge strain on the marriage when they are all taken on and quickly adopted. Add to that the fact that the wife is now dressing and acting differently, the couple's group of friends change – because of kosher eating habits or new interests – and activities that used to be so simple, such as going to a movie, are now viewed in a different light.

The dynamic of the whole relationship changes. Husband and wife take on new and unaccustomed roles as they explore new territories. It is easy to see how a husband – even a man who *wants* to be more observant – can have problems if the changes occur too abruptly or without his complete understanding and consent. This was the problem which my beloved husband and I found ourselves facing.

Quite early on we agreed to fully observe the Shabbat, which was a major adjustment. It meant that we would no longer do "creative" work on that day: cooking, driving or riding, chores or even recreational activities like ball games or gardening. On the seventh day we rest from "creative" work in observance of the seventh day on which G-d Himself rested after creating the universe. Saturdays were different, replaced with delightful walks to the synagogue, a light lunch there after the three-hour service, and the rest of the day spent in the company of friends and family. Withdrawing from the hustle and busy work of the week allowed us to be more aware of G-d and enjoy the greater sense of closeness unique to that day. But this change was relatively easy to agree on.

We were also in agreement about raising our level of observance of the kosher laws. Our kitchen was already kosher, but it was now raised to a higher level of compliance with the requirements for complete separation of meat and milk products — includes three sets of dishes and cookware and countless other minor manifestations that can be both puzzling and frustrating when one first begins. No problem there, as we had always kept these laws, albeit on a less intense level.

Similarly – and this particularly delighted me – finally he was agreedto further our existing observance of the laws of Family Purity, which involve a husband and wife refraining from intimacy (or even touching) during the woman's menstrual period and for seven days thereafter. Family Purity can be a big point of contention for a couple becoming more observant. For obvious reasons, there can be serious problems in the relationship if a couple is not in perfect agreement on this one.

These mitzvahs were not a source of contention for us. It was a few of the remaining mitzvahs that caused us problems — like my wearing a wig, for one. A married woman is required to conceal her hair from everyone but her husband. Some married women wear hats, scarves or other kinds of hair coverings, but many wear wigs — very attractive wigs, in most cases, but wigs nonetheless.

I wanted all the mitzvahs, all at once — wig included. Some husbands object. Mine was one of them. He objected. Seriously objected. Domestic Tranquility, another mitzvah, was obviously impacted by the dispute.

In my mind, all I wanted was to keep everything — and that included wearing a wig. To me it was simple. This was a requirement established by G-d that helps ensure proper modesty among Jewish women. I couldn't understand my husband's objections. Couldn't he see this was a mitzvah I was required to keep? How could he not agree?

There was conflict in our home. Once again I turned to the Rebbe who had started us on this journey by participating in my husband's cure. Now, we needed his help to move forward. I wrote and handed a long and detailed letter, all the while confident the Rebbe would say, "Of course you must follow the law and wear a wig no matter what your husband says!"

I had a lot to learn about the Rebbe.

Instead of urging me on and taking "my side," so to speak, the letter encouraged me to have patience, to do as many of the mitzvahs as I was able, but, above all, to keep peace in our home. The Rebbe was telling me – and on many more occasions repeated the message – that maintaining Domestic Tranquility took precedence in this case, yet I still struggled.

One day I could take it no more. "I'm wearing a wig," I thought. "I was commanded by G-d to do so, and I need to keep this mitzvah!" I decided to go ahead, buy a wig, put it on and let everyone adjust. Anyone who objected would just have to come to terms with the new me.

I wrote to inform the Rebbe of my decision: "I have decided I am going to buy and wear a wig. Both friends and various rabbis have encouraged me to do so, and I am going ahead. I see no reason to wait any longer. I am sure you agree that a Jew should keep *all* the mitzvahs, and I'm asking for your blessing as I begin to keep this one."

It felt strange when I didn't receive a prompt answer from the Rebbe as I had become accustomed. Until that point, the Rebbe had always answered me very quickly, and I had come to depend a great deal on his advice and counsel. Why wouldn't he answer me on this matter? Why was there no blessing for my increased observance? What could be the problem? I waited anxiously for two days.

Finally, my answer arrived in the mail, a cryptic one-sentence response: "What will you tell your husband when he asks you what the reason for this change is?" asked the Rebbe.

And then I understood.

The mitzvah of maintaining Domestic Tranquility called for a peace between my husband and I in which we could grow *together,* and it was more important than my moving ahead on my own. At that juncture, the Rebbe was more concerned with the success of our marriage than with my observance of a specific mitzvah that caused tension. He was telling me, again, to be patient. And he was, of course, absolutely correct.

There were many times of conflict in our marriage — which couple doesn't have such times? But I was learning a new perspective. The Rebbe taught and ingrained within me a very important principle: marriage was instituted by G-d to unite one soul and two bodies. The Torah doesn't see a couple as two separate creatures, male and female. Rather, the vision is of a married couple as a fully completed being, a single unit with a male and a female component. It is far more important that the single unit survive intact than that it self-destructs so that one part can better itself.

I had to learn this all-important lesson through experience. But that's the object of a story, obviously: to learn from other peoples' lives and apply what you've learned to your own life.

I invite you to learn from my experience, as I have learned from the experience of so many others.

Words To Hear With Your Heart

I will never forget the first time I met with the Rebbe face-to-face. I treasure every minute spent in the Rebbe's room, and the merit my family and I had to speak with him privately.

It was in 1981, on the occasion of my son, David Yechezkel's, bar mitzvah. He was born on the fifth of the Hebrew month of Shevat. In Lubavitch, the tenth day of Shevat marks the anniversary of the Rebbe's taking on the leadership of Chabad. Thus, our meeting also served as an opportunity to pay respect to the Rebbe for his leadership.

When the Rebbe would hold private meetings, the number of people seeking an appointment was so great that one-on-one sessions would frequently go on through the night, and then the Rebbe would work a full day, just as though he had slept. We were lucky — our appointment was for 11 p.m. When it was our turn, my husband and I, our children and my parents – who had flown in from Israel for the occasion – were all ushered into the Rebbe's private office.

Now, you have to understand where we were at that time, in terms of observance. This was during the time that my husband and I were in great disagreement – to say the least – about my wholehearted enthusiasm for the Torah's mitzvahs, and my husband's strongly disapproving attitude. So you are free to assume that I was anxious and tense about the meeting. For myself, I wanted nothing more than to be able to meet with the Rebbe, listen to every word he spoke, and treasure them for the rest of my life. At the same time, I was concerned about how the rest of the family was going to handle it all.

I will never forget the feeling as I stepped into that holy space and saw the Rebbe behind his desk. I imagined the countless encounters, words spoken, emotions felt and deep connections forged in that room throughout the years. First, the Rebbe stood up, greeted us and graciously bade us to take a seat, gesturing with his hand toward the chair opposite him as he returned to his. In English he asked us when and where the upcoming bar mitzvah would be held.

Then the Rebbe turned to Benjamin, who was standing right next to him, and said the following, very slowly, and emphatically, all the while looking him straight in the eye: "If you help people go in G-d's way, then you will be doing G-d's work and be standing in His place. Accordingly, if you do this, then G-d will respond by helping in *your* work and you will receive riches, more than you ever thought possible."

The Rebbe stared at Benjamin, and the words seemed to echo off the wall and hang in the air. The Rebbe pierced the silence when he asked Benjamin if he had understood what was said. Trust me, no one who has been on the receiving end of the Rebbe's steady, penetrating gaze can ever come up with an intelligent answer to that question. My hapless husband merely stammered something vague.

"I will repeat it," the Rebbe said, and proceeded to do precisely that, word for word, every bit as slowly and emphatically as he had the first time. When he had finished, he looked long and hard at my husband, and then added, "I hope that you have heard with your heart as well as your head."

There was a long moment of silence.

He then turned to all of us and extended a general blessing. As the Rebbe proceeded to hand each of us in turn one crisp new dollar bill, he smilingly explained, "On these occasions I permit myself to give dollars to all the family." It was the Rebbe's frequent custom to give dollars to inspire the recipients to give charity. The Rebbe's hand extending across the table is forever emblazoned on my mind. I can replay the words, how courteously he phrased it — "permitting" himself to give us dollars, as if we were doing something for him! The Rebbe blessed all of us again, and it was time for us to leave.

Walking out the door, I could not stop smiling and shivering with awe and happiness. The whole night I couldn't sleep. I wanted to literally dance and jump for joy! Since that time I heard it expressed many times, that the Rebbe's prescription for drawing someone else closer, to anything, is best accomplished by making them the influencer of others. The Rebbe knew of our situation then, and his words to my husband were extremely effective to this very day, thank G-d.

What was the result? Well, for one thing, the Rebbe had phrased his words perfectly, as always. He had empowered my husband to be influential and the decision-maker. Our marital challenges were not solved overnight, but they were enormously improved and – together with my greater concentration on maintaining Domestic Tranquility – were eventually resolved. Major issues that had once felt like a raging river were first reduced to a tiny stream, and eventually to an occasional trickle. Because he knew us both, because he knew G-d's will for us both and because he took the time to care, the Rebbe profoundly helped us both.

The restoration of peace in our home was a deal brokered by the Rebbe — a very successful deal, indeed.

Ancestral Values Rediscovered

In retrospect, it seems odd to me that I struggled to perceive the primacy of peace. I had every cultural reason to have learned the lessons of Domestic Tranquility much more easily.

As I mentioned, I come from the Iranian Jewish community of Mashhad. It's a Persian community famous for its close-knit, traditional lives in which members tended to marry only within their own ranks.

This tradition results from a history of persecution in Iran. In the mid-1800's, the infamous Allah Dadi pogrom took place. The Muslims of Mashhad threatened to massacre the Jews if they did not convert to Islam. Forty Jews were killed, and the sages of the community decided that they had to save themselves from death. So the Jews pretended to go along with the demand, but, much like the Conversos of Spain – sometimes called "marranos" by their tormentors, a word that means "swine" – they continued their Jewish practices in secret.

One of the solutions they found to ensure that their children would never, G-d forbid, convert was to ensure that their children married only within the fold. The only way they could do this was to betroth their children to a specific mate at a very young age — sometimes even at birth. Then, if a Muslim asked for a young woman's hand in marriage, the parents would say, "Oh, no, we are sorry. She is already betrothed to someone else!" And the Muslims, fearing Allah, would respect this. They would never take a girl promised to someone else. And so the hidden Jews of Mashhad were able to maintain their scrupulously Jewish life, all accomplished in secret, in order to save their very lives.

Now, what about those marriages designated at birth — were they successful? Remarkably so. What about compatibility, you ask? They *made* themselves compatible, even though there must have been great differences in a couple betrothed from birth!

Divorce in Jewish Mashhad was virtually unknown. The parties to a marriage firmly believed they were destined for each other. That being the case, each partner simply accepted, as a fact of life, that the spouse was chosen by G-d for life, with no space for doubt. The women endured great adversities, keeping a perfectly observant Jewish life in complete secret — making Passover matzahs, keeping kosher, maintaining Family Purity and observing the Shabbat without any outsider knowing. Each one was a modest woman of valor who accomplished everything with so much grace, dignity and love of G-d.

If I had just kept in mind the idea that my husband was indeed my destined mate – the other half of my very self, the one chosen by G-d to be my partner forever – I would have learned my lesson from the saga of my own people. If I'd really understood that, of course I would have put peace in the home first.

It just took me longer than the Rebbe, but eventually I did see it.

Much later, when I finally began to put a priority on peace in our home, my husband became more supportive and our individual paths to observance began to converge.

With Sensitivity To All

After our first private audience, my husband would not go to the Rebbe for many years.

I realize now that he probably felt threatened and thought that "they" were "brainwashing" his wife and taking me away from him. After all, I was the one who had changed, not him.

However, one special day my husband actually agreed to come to "Dollars" with me. The Rebbe established a custom of greeting thousands of people on Sundays, standing for hours as the seemingly endless line of people passed by the podium near his office. Some passed by silently, content to see and be seen by the Rebbe and receive a dollar bill, like we had in our private meeting. Others sought advice, or wished to share important news or introduce family and friends. In effect, it was an hours-long demonstration of the spiritual power of giving.

On this Sunday, "Dollars" took place at the Rebbe's home, due to it being within the year of mourning after the passing of the Rebbetzin, Chaya Mushka Schneerson. This day, my mother had come to visit us from Israel, and she asked Benjamin to come with us when I took her to the Rebbe for Dollars. My husband, thank G-d, has great respect for my mother and is so fond of her that he can refuse her nothing. (I try to emulate her in my relationships with my own sons-in-law. It works!)

When our turn finally arrived, I stepped forward and told the Rebbe, "This is my husband," gesturing to him. The Rebbe turned to my husband with a beaming smile. "Your name is Binyomin," he said to him, taking him by surprise because his name was never mentioned in front of the Rebbe. He went on to tell him the meaning of his name, and earnestly added, "If you help Mrs. Karmely in her activities, she will cooperate with you in religious observances. May Almighty G-d bless you and your family in everything!"

We hardly had time to get over this when it was my mother's turn to receive a dollar. "This is my mother," I said as I introduced her. Again the Rebbe turned with a huge beaming smile, and, pointing to me, said to her, "Thank you for producing such a daughter!" My mother opened her mouth to speak, but no words could come out. Instead, she burst into tears, overwhelmed and touched. The Rebbe kept smiling as he gave her a dollar and a blessing.

What a lesson! What does one tell a mother? The one thing she needs to hear: you raised a child the right way. I appreciate so much that the Rebbe made my mother proud and joyous. It was unforgettable.

That very next Sunday, I again went to the Rebbe for Dollars. (I used to take groups of people I had met at my talks to the Rebbe.)

When my turn came, the Rebbe asked me kindly, "What was your husband's reaction after last week?" He waited for an answer.

I could not speak, as my heart was so full. I felt that I too, like my mother, would burst into tears, that the Rebbe actually remembered all my troubles and took the time to ask me. After a few moments the Rebbe gently nodded, saying, "It will be better the next time." He then gave me beautiful blessings and the usual dollars for myself, my husband and my activities.

The Rebbe showed us what it means to love and to care. How grateful I am to him, for guiding me and showing me the right path, like a patient and wise father.

ℒ

The hardest thing for me to write about was the time when I went to the Rebbe for Dollars and he told me something very powerful.

As I have mentioned, I did not realize how difficult it would be for my husband to accept the change in my lifestyle. I wanted to keep every mitzvah one thousand percent. After all, didn't I have to make up for lost time? I saw my husband's disapproval and lack of cooperation (to put it mildly) as a millstone around my neck, and I deeply resented it.

One Sunday at Dollars, the Rebbe gave me his usual happy smile and my three dollars: "One for your activities, one for you, and one for your husband *so he should not be angry with me.*" I thought I was hearing wrong. The line pressed forward and I was halfway out the door. I blurted out, "What?!" The Rebbe turned to me, still smiling, and repeated, "For your husband, *so that he should not be angry with me.*"

I left the building dazed and slowly backed away, not knowing what to say or do. As I turned to go, it hit me what the Rebbe had told me. He was gently telling me that I was the one who was turning my poor, long-suffering husband against the Rebbe and Judaism by pushing to keep every single mitzvah, right away, at the expense of his feelings.

After crying in the arms of my friend, Mrs. Gitlin, who was there, I went home and resolved to be more sensitive to my husband and not cram Judaism and Chabad down his throat.

I had to learn the hard way, but those embarking on a Torah-observant life often mistakenly change personalities or become strangers to their families by making Judaism his or her family. Instead, by being understanding of our spouses, parents, siblings and children, our Judaism becomes a true sanctification of Hashem, and encourages others to follow because they see its beauty.

Despair And Renewal

Years ago there was a point in my marriage when I actually told the Rebbe that I couldn't handle it anymore. "G-d forbid, G-d forbid," he answered.

However, as the years went by, things did not improve much. My husband refused to even talk to me about covering my hair; it flew in the face of his ideology. He thought I was crazy to be "different" — surely it sufficed to wear a hat only when I went to synagogue! Every time I would hear someone complain about how hard it was to wear a wig, I felt like bursting out, "You are so lucky! Just appreciate the fact that you can!" My husband also refused to budge on other issues.

I wanted to live as a Jewish woman should, and believed that I would feel more peace and tranquility by leaving. I wrote this to the Rebbe, also mentioning that my good friends advised me to do so as well.

The answer came in a long, inspiring letter. The Rebbe quoted the language of a Jewish marriage ceremony and asked how I could possibly feel tranquil and at peace with separating from my husband when we had been married "according to the laws of Moshe and Israel"? Moreover, he said, women and girls around me look up to me as an example, and I influence them positively. He blessed me that I should take my children to the wedding canopy from a peaceful and complete home, with both parents together. After writing that he would pray for me, as well as other words of encouragement, the Rebbe wrote that I should wait until my last child got married and then "we would see."

I carried this beautiful letter around with me for fifteen years. It gave me strength in trying times. I only kept going because of the Rebbe and his kindness and concern.

In 1996, the issue of wearing a wig was raised again. My dear father, who lived in Israel, passed on and I chose to turn the negative into something positive. I told my husband that for the whole year that I was in the prerequisite mourning period for my father, I intended to cover my hair as a gesture of respect. I knew that this was something he could understand and accept. He went along with this, on the condition that it should be a head covering such as a hat, but not a wig. I went along with this condition, hoping that as time passed my husband would become accustomed to me covering my hair. I wore my wig whenever my husband was not around and hats when he was.

As the year was drawing to a close, I started to panic — it was now or never. I had to take a stand and go forward. But how could I do so and still have Domestic Tranquility? One month before the mourning period ended, my youngest daughter, Daniella Miriam, got engaged. We planned an engagement celebration for our daughter in our synagogue's ballroom. I would be wearing a gown and had my wig ready.

I dreaded the confrontation that I feared my husband would make at the event when he would see me in my wig. What could I do?

I needed my rock and reached out for a connection to the Rebbe and put it on his shoulders. It was 1998, four years after the Rebbe's passing. My weekly custom had become to visit the Rebbe's grave site. This time, I made a special visit very late at night and waited until I was alone with the Rebbe.

I cried, pouring out my heart and soul. "You told me things would be different after my last daughter got married. You said that I should wait. You said we'll see then. So? I waited, and now is the time! Help me! How much longer?"

Leaving the grave site, I felt so much lighter — as if my burden was now on stronger shoulders. Nonetheless, I was not prepared for what ensued the following day.

Without warning or explanation, my husband turned to me and said, "Well, now, I suppose you're going to wear a wig for the party?" I just stood there, speechless. I could not answer, but just nodded in stunned silence.

Although my husband was not complimentary (to put it mildly) about how I looked in my wig, he now accepted it. My prayers had been answered, thank G-d.

He Spoke Her Language

I was once speaking with a dear friend about the experience of having a private audience with the Rebbe. She shared with me what transpired many years ago when she went with her then future husband for a private audience with the Rebbe.

At that time she had not yet quite mastered Yiddish. However, she spoke English and Hebrew well. Her groom, who did speak Yiddish, urged her to ask the Rebbe to speak to her in Yiddish. "But I don't understand it," she said. He continued to insist, explaining that he wanted the Rebbe to speak to her in Yiddish since he always led Chassidic gatherings in that language. Reluctantly, she capitulated.

As soon as they entered the room, the Rebbe held up his hand to the groom, motioning him to not speak yet, and turned to my friend. In a firm, yet kindly voice, *in English,* he asked her, "Which language would you like me to speak, English or Hebrew?"

My friend, taken aback by the unexpected question, forgot about what her groom had asked her to do and blurted out, "Hebrew!"

The Rebbe spoke with her in that holy tongue, and only

after that did he turn to the groom and speak to him in Yiddish.

How did he know? Oh, we have so much to learn from the Rebbe!

On Coincidence

"Coincidence"

The Hebrew language lacks a word for "coincidence," which demonstrates that random occurrences, as such, are simply not a part of Jewish thinking. Absolutely everything we experience happens for a reason.

One of the most delightful Chassidic stories I know is told about a rebbe, the Baal Shem Tov, walking along a country road. Enjoying the warm day and the greenery around him, he observed a leaf detach from an overhanging branch and drift down to the ground in the breeze. "Why did You cause that leaf to fall?" he spontaneously asked G-d. "Pick up the leaf," G-d responded. The Baal Shem Tov moved closer and retrieved the leaf, only to find a small worm underneath that had been too hot in the sun and needed shade to survive. "See?" said G-d. "The worm asked Me to help, so I arranged for the wind to rustle the branches, remove the leaf and drop it right where it was needed most."

We learn a profound lesson from the story. If G-d can care so deeply about such a tiny creature, think how much He cares about us! Everything that happens to us – yes everything – is arranged by G-d for the specific purpose of drawing us closer to Him. Some of the most astonishing stories I've heard are those that result from "coincidence." Often, they are seemingly random events which are actually thinly veiled messages from G-d; invitations to see Him in His world, to recognize His existence and to lovingly bring us closer. Here are a few of the stories that have come my way, reminding again and again how much G-d cares about each one of His people, wherever they are, whatever they are doing.

Rosie On The Train

In this frenetic era, people, and especially women, juggle more and more demands with less and less time. I'm no exception. I once saw a bumper sticker: "I Am Woman, I Am Invincible, I Am Tired!" At one point, I was balancing speaking, teaching and a day job in Manhattan as a gemologist, as well as taking care of a home and family.

One fine day after work I got on the subway to go home to Queens. As usual, the subway was crowded, but I finally found a seat and took out my little prayer book to finish reading the day's Psalms. As I read, I could feel someone's eyes on me — hardly unusual in that situation. I chose to ignore it and continued reading. After a time, curiosity got the better of me and I looked around to see my audience. A young woman was sitting several seats away, close enough to look, but too far to talk. I kept reading until my stop arrived and departed the train. A few steps out the door I felt a tap on my shoulder and turned to see the young woman from the train. Smiling slightly, she asked in Hebrew, "Are you from Chabad?" I smiled and said that yes, I was.

"I saw you reading from your prayer book," she explained somewhat awkwardly, and introduced herself as Rosie. "I could see it was a Chabad prayer book." We began to talk, and she eagerly told me her story.

Rosie had lived in Israel for a time and had come to know Chabad there. But, after returning to New York, she had gradually drifted away from Judaism and a Jewish way of life, eventually abandoning all forms of Jewish observance. As she became more and more involved in secular activities, she began to yearn for some of the warmth, love and satisfaction she had felt in Israel when she was involved with a Jewish community, living and growing in the observance of the mitzvahs. Unfortunately, the secular cave she had built was isolating her from observant Jews. She wanted to "come home," she said, but had no idea where or how to start. The night before, she went on, she had felt very lost and lonely. In tears she had had prayed to G-d: "Please, I want to come back. Please send me someone to give me some guidance, to tell me how and where I should look. I need to know how to live as a Jew." Then she had cried herself to sleep.

The next day she saw me on the train, reading from the Chabad prayer book. This was her answer, she thought — the thing she had prayed for.

Was this a coincidence? To my mind – and Rosie's – certainly not! For Rosie, it was the beginning of a new life. I was touched by her sincerity, and I wanted to help. We found Hebrew-language classes for Rosie at her local Chabad center about the basics of Judaism, and she became involved with a new group of observant friends. She was on her way. And me? I got to see, one more time, that there is no such thing as coincidence.

The Mystery Of The Lost Address Book

Divine Providence is the idea that everything which happens in the world is G-d's Will and full of purpose and meaning. Sometimes, it can take each of us countless experiences before it begins to sink in that what seems at the moment to be a problem, burden or "bad," is actually just a part of a very good thing which we will ultimately be grateful for and appreciate. As our Sages say, every descent is for the sake of an ascent. The descent, while perhaps uncomfortable, is actually a crucial part of the subsequent ascent — the beginning. *Every* descent? Of course — even such a mundane thing as a lost address book.

One evening, after work in Manhattan, I planned to attend a class at a synagogue where Rabbi Manis Friedman was scheduled to speak. Rabbi Friedman is world-renowned author, counselor, lecturer and philosopher whose captivating style makes Jewish mysticism accessible to everyone. Over the years, he has become one of my closest advisers. As early as possible I rushed out of the office and hopped into a taxi to make sure I would get to the synagogue on time — only to discover that I had either lost or misplaced my address book. Was it in the office? Did I drop it in the street? There I was, in the taxi, going somewhere, but I no longer knew where that destination was. Without that address book, I wasn't sure what to tell the taxi driver.

I did vaguely remember the location – not quite good enough in New York – so I gave the driver a general idea of where I wanted to stop and he let me out. There I was, not too sure where I was or where I needed to go, and alone in Manhattan. "This too is for the good," I tried to coach myself as I stood there puzzled and unsure which direction to pick. It was then that I saw a Jewish-looking couple walking up the street and decided to ask them for help.

"Excuse me," I began. "Do you know of a synagogue around here?"

"Which one?" the woman asked. "There are several of them, actually."

"Oh … well, I can't remember the name, and I must have left my address book in the office, but Rabbi Manis Friedman is speaking there tonight and …"

I guess my voice trailed off as I ran out of information.

She was an elegant, aristocratic-looking lady who was being awfully nice to this lost woman who wanted to find a place for which she had neither name nor address. That is not, to say the least, typical of most New Yorkers! This very impressive lady, however, sent her husband off home – they lived in the area, she said – and volunteered to help me find the place. She began telling me her background as we walked off together: her name was Sarah (same as mine!), she was Jewish, British-born (almost like me!), had an eleven-year-old daughter, owned her own New York literary agency, and was completely nonobservant, a fact that she revealed in the same voice in which she might report the weather.

In that way that women have, I quickly told her a little about myself and why I was going to hear Rabbi Friedman. He would be speaking on the mitzvah of Family Purity, I explained, and it would surely have great meaning.

Then, suddenly, I was inspired.

"Come with me!" I said. "You'll enjoy it — I promise this will be different from anything you've been to before!"

"Oh, but I can't," she said. "I really know nothing at all about Judaism. Our home was not observant at all. In fact, the last time I was in a synagogue was more than ten years ago when I visited India (where I was born!), and stopped in a small synagogue on Rosh Hashanah. No, I really can't, I'd be embarrassed at my ignorance."

By this time we had walked around the block, and – finally – saw other people walking purposefully toward something, which I figured must be the lecture. Miraculously, the synagogue I was looking for was just around the corner from where the taxi had let me off. And what's more, Sarah's daughter went to a school just across the street. She had no idea there was even a synagogue in this building. I kept repeating both my thanks and my invitation, and finally Sarah agreed to come in — but just for five minutes.

"Fine," I said, confident that no one can ever listen to Rabbi Friedman for just five minutes. Of course, Sarah stayed for the whole program, and the talk – a unique presentation of powerful spiritual truths interspersed with warm, delightful humor – won her over.

Not long after, Sarah and her family came to our home for Shabbat dinner, an evening I will never forget. One of the most precious gifts I've received from G-d is having the opportunity to see the joy and radiance that comes over a Jewish woman's face when she celebrates Shabbat for the first time. There is nothing so rewarding as seeing the blossoming of the Jewish soul as it is touched by the holiness of the Shabbat. Sarah fell in love with the Shabbat candles I use – olive oil with homemade wicks — and the next time I saw her, I brought enough glass holders and wicks for both Sarah and her daughter. Sarah started coming to a regular Chabad class with me, asking lots of questions and growing day by day. Eventually, I taught her the secret of rich, rewarding marriages: Family Purity — the cycle of union and separation between husband and wife that is predicated on the woman's monthly cycle and culminates with her immersion in a *mikvah,* or ritual bath. The whole family is now growing together in observance.

And Sarah now has stories of her own. Her daughter, in that public school so close to the synagogue, had been part of a class that was scheduled to go on a field trip to a cathedral where they would be singing non-Jewish songs. Not exactly the place for a nice Jewish girl! But with her new knowledge of who and what she is, the daughter stood up and proclaimed that she was

Jewish and could not go. To her surprise, another girl stood up and said she, too, was Jewish, and also refused to participate. Thank G-d, both were allowed to remain home instead of going on that field trip.

There will be more "Sarah stories," I know, and more about her brave little girl — all due to the fact that one evening, as I was leaving work, G-d momentarily blocked my vision and I didn't see the address book left lying on my desk!

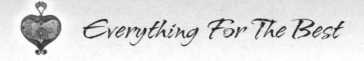

Everything For The Best

Surely one of the most frequent tests we have in this world is dealing with what appears to be disappointment.

In the midst of what seems like defeat, it's hard to remember that everything is always for the best. G-d, who stands outside of time and utterly beyond its limitations, can see our individual paths with perfect clarity. Our vision, on the other hand, is strictly limited. From time to time we all struggle with situations that seem to be problematic, even minor irritations: an appointment cancelled, a meeting missed due to traffic, a picnic rained out. And yet most of these little disturbances, once the event has passed and our view has changed to retrospective, are revealed as having been major blessings all along.

Life is full of such experiences. One time I heard that the Rebbe would be distributing specially printed booklets of one of his essays to inspire the learning of its timely message. This is an uncommon event in Lubavitch that attracts attention greater than a book signing by the superstar author of the latest best-seller. It was to be held on an evening when I could attend. I was delighted – I could hardly ever go to evening events – and I definitely planned to go.

However, I had another event that same night, something I also wanted very much to go to. One of the brides from my marriage preparation classes was having the traditional Sephardic "henna" party — a lovely traditional event for women only that takes place just before a wedding. But I figured out a way I could do both. In talking to a member of the Rebbe's staff, I was told that the event would be starting very late, so I could go to the henna party first, and when that was over, I could still make it in time to the Rebbe and receive a booklet from his holy hand.

I went to the party and enjoyed myself thoroughly. At around 10 p.m. I called the Rebbe's office to see how much longer I might be able to stay. To my surprise, I was told that the Rebbe's event was already over! I was so disappointed — it was such a rare occasion when I could actually get to one of those events. Upset, I did my best to remember that everything G-d does is for the best, and went back to the ladies at the party.

One of the women there was named Gila. I decided to chat with her awhile, since I was no longer running to the Rebbe. As it turned out, she had all sorts of issues that she needed to discuss with someone. When we finally parted after 1 a.m., I thought I understood why G-d had wanted me at that party: I was able to offer Gila some reassurance.

The next morning, I heard the shocking news: during the night, Gila's husband – a young man and father of their three children (the youngest only seven!) – had passed away peacefully in his sleep. I felt so sorry for Gila and the children, but there was a blessing, too. Because of the long talk we'd had and the warm feelings we had developed for each other, Gila felt able to call on me to help her through the terrible pain and suffering of losing a husband so unexpectedly. Specifically, she was heartened to learn about two fundamental tenets of the Jewish faith: the belief in the ultimate redemption of the Jewish people – and of all of mankind – through a righteous Moshaich (Messiah), and the concept of the Resurrection of the Dead, an awaited time when all souls will return to their bodies.

After a period of adjustment, Gila told me she had decided that what was now important to her was that she and her children become Torah observant.

It would be presumptuous of me to suggest that we ever know why G-d decides to collect those souls that He does, when He does. The fact that the Rebbe's event ended early that evening meant that I had the time to come to know Gila, and even though I was terribly disappointed at missing the chance to see the Rebbe, I now more clearly see what G-d had in mind for me that evening!

So when apparently irritating and bothersome events or missed opportunities befall us, keep in mind that we are not seeing the whole picture. While it seems that we failed to achieve and accomplish what we thought was best for us, the real purpose of the "failure" usually remains unknown. I'm always so grateful when G-d lifts the curtain, lets me connect the dots, and – if only for a split second – get a glimpse of the big picture He envisioned from the beginning.

A "Coincidental" Neighbor

There was a lovely Israeli lady in her twenties named Tamar who lived in our apartment building in Kew Gardens, Queens. Tamar was sweet and kind, very spiritual in her own way, but not at all interested in Torah or mitzvahs. I suppose the reason was that no one in her circle of friends was observant, and so it probably just seemed unnecessary or too difficult. Not that I didn't try: she came to a Shabbat meal at our home and loved it; I took her to the *mikvah* and she loved that too — although cutting her fingernails and having to re-curl her lovely hair was too stressful for her to want to do it again. Nor was she interested in keeping Shabbat. "What would I do all day?" she asked. "I'd be so bored!"

But where I had failed to ignite the spark, my daughters Esther and Miriam succeeded. My daughters and their circle of friends, also in their twenties, are all Torah-observant and it seemed natural for them to invite Tamar to be with them — not that they pressured her, or even had any ulterior motives. They thought she was an interesting person and they wanted her to be a part of their group. And Tamar responded. She started by joining their weekly get-together with all their children – a fun evening with its quotient of girl-talk – and progressed pretty quickly to being a regular part of the crowd. At first she was self-conscious about her lack of knowledge and seemed a little defensive, but that passed quickly as her knowledge increased. No better way to learn how to keep a kosher house than to watch your best friends doing it!

One morning Tamar stopped me in the halwayl to tell me how happy she was that she had decided to become observant of the Shabbat — and also to keep kosher. I was absolutely delighted, although it would have been difficult for my joy to have exceeded hers.

I asked why she had made this decision.

"It was Esther, Miriam and their friends," she said. "They are all so good — they are *good* to me and to each other. And I started to envy them — they are all so much happier than my other friends. No gossip and no backstabbing. Anyway, I really admired them. I wanted to be like them — no, it was more that I wanted to *be* them! And I knew I could, if I tried hard enough!"

And there was another factor, too. Tamar had finally had a much-desired baby boy, after two beautiful girls. "I wanted, somehow, to pay G-d back for all the goodness He has given me," she said. "The least I could do would be to do the things He has already asked me to do!"

Tamar is now setting an example for her old friends. Several of her nonobservant Israeli friends are seeing Tamar's new contentment, and wondering if they could have some of that for themselves. No problem there!

The "Coincidence" Of A Name

While in Bangkok on a business trip, my husband and I went to a large department store looking for some souvenirs to bring back for friends. As we were getting out of our taxi, we saw a young man on the street wearing a large black yarmulke. Hardly a common sight in Bangkok! We started to talk – instant friends in that exotic locale – and I kept thinking that he looked very familiar, although I couldn't imagine where I would have met him before. We parted with the good feeling you get from having run into a brother so far from everything that is familiar.

I did have a good friend in Bangkok, a woman named Sonya, and the next morning Sonya and I sat down for a time. I couldn't resist telling her about the observant young man we had met on the street yesterday — but midway through the story, Sonya started to laugh. She'd already heard the story, she said. The young man was her brother Moshe — he must have looked familiar to me because he looked like her! Eventually, we spent more time with Moshe and heard his story.

Moshe had been totally nonobservant, living in Israel and, after coming within a hair of marrying a non-Jewish German girl, had decided to leave and go to the Far East to make his fortune. He soon found himself in Bangkok.

One day – it was Saturday, the Jewish Shabbat – he went

downtown to go shopping at that very same department store where we had initially met. As he walked down the street, doing some people-watching, a thought struck him like a thunderbolt. He saw how the Asian people would stop and bow down to their idols each time they saw one, or even caught a glimpse of one, and he was impressed. If they were completely unembarrassed to stop and bow down before a piece of stone or metal, he thought, what did that say about a Jew who was embarrassed to even wear a yarmulke in respect to the Creator of the world? "My name is Moshe," he thought. "Am I living up to that name?"

He decided right then and there, in front of all the idols, that like the original Moses he would recognize his Creator; he would be an observant Jew. If these people were unafraid to show their devotion to wood and stone, how could he, who knew the Creator of those materials, fail to show at least some respect?

Moshe lived up to his word. He began to keep Shabbat and kosher laws – not an easy thing to do in Bangkok! – and began to study the Torah at every opportunity. Now, he gives classes in the synagogue on Shabbat, and speaks with great pride of his holy Moroccan ancestors. He believes it was the spiritual power of his name – Moshe – that had been dormant, waiting for a spark to ignite it. And what did G-d use to set this Jewish soul ablaze? Stone and metal images, idols — things that are abhorrent to Jews!

G-d can use *anything* in His creation for His purposes — even things like idols that are the epitome of evil.

Yaakov And The Mitzvah Of Keeping Kosher

A distant cousin of my Father, Yaakov, told me his story, a powerful tribute to a remarkable "coincidence."

It happened in Iran, just after the revolution in 1979, when thousands of people were desperately trying to get out of the country. It had become very dangerous to remain in Iran, but getting out was equally dangerous and was growing increasingly difficult. Yaakov had managed to send his wife and children out to safety, but he himself needed to stay a little longer to try to salvage some of his business assets. Unfortunately, by the time he was ready to go, leaving was verging on the impossible: very few flights and exit visas were being given out at what seemed to be the whim of the bureaucrats. The only thing people could do was go to the airport every day and hope for permission to leave from the customs officials — and then hope to find a seat on any plane to anywhere at the same time. Iran was in total anarchy at that time. Nothing was organized, and people haphazardly took flights at the whims of the mullahs in charge.

When all else failed, Yaakov tried this method, too. Every day he packed a few items he intended to take with him out of the country and went to the airport, prepared to spend all day watching, waiting and hoping for an opening somewhere.

One day, after having spent almost a dozen hours haggling with bureaucrats and airline officials to no avail, he saw some non-Jewish friends of his who were also trying to leave. They too had been stymied, and as the last flight out for the day roared down the runway, they decided they may as well get something to eat.

Now, Yaakov will tell you he was not a completely observant Jew, but one mitzvah that he did keep scrupulously was eating kosher. So, when his friends suggested they go to the very nice airport restaurant on the second floor, he said he couldn't go. It was not kosher, he said, and as much as he would like to sit and talk with friends who were also enduring this horrific experience, he really couldn't eat in that restaurant. Someone suggested another idea — why didn't they just go to the airport snack bar instead, the one on the first floor? They had sandwiches and salads there, he said, and surely there would be something Yaakov could eat. Again Yaakov, tired and hungry as he was, had to say no. "There is more to keeping kosher than just meat," he said. "I can't eat at the snack bar either." But then he had an idea, "Why don't you come to my home? There's still some food there, and I'll cook. Then we can relax in comfort, and we can all eat." They only hesitated a minute before accepting his invitation, and they all enjoyed the evening at Yaakov's home enormously.

The next morning they heard the news. The night before – just after they had all left the airport – there had been a massive building collapse in the building in which the airport's restaurants were located. Years before, when the restaurant was being renovated, construction officials had taken out the two main pillars that provided support. On the day Yaakov's friends had urged him to eat with them in those restaurants, the strain had finally been too much and the building collapsed. Dozens of people were killed and hundreds were injured as three floors of debris fell into the restaurant on the lower level. Most of the people who had been in the two restaurants had died.

Needless to say, keeping kosher is still one mitzvah that Yaakov never even thinks of compromising! His friends are still telling the story of how "the G-d of the Jews" saved them all from death just because their Jewish friend was careful about obeying G-d's Law!

A Jewish Mechanic

There is no limit to the number of miracles that G-d works every day. Some are major personal miracles like Yaakov's. Others are the kind that leave you shaking your head in joy and laughter, delighting in how far G-d will go to take care of you.

One such incident took place not too long ago, when my husband and I, together with our children, were returning from a family bar mitzvah on Long Island. We were having so much fun that we stayed to the very end of the festivities and found ourselves leaving for Queens at 3:30 a.m.! The kids and I were exhausted, and we promptly fell asleep in the car, leaving my poor husband to do the driving all by himself.

Some time later, I was shaken awake when our car came to a quick stop. I saw the panicked look on my husband's face, and knew that our car – which had been acting up a little – had decided to take this moment, in these early morning hours far from home, to stop altogether. Worse yet, we had come to a stop in a very dangerous place — there wasn't much of a shoulder to pull off on and huge trucks were whizzing by, making our car shiver and shake in their wake. And, there was no phone in sight; this was in the 1980s, before cell phones.

In a break in traffic, my husband and son jumped out to try to push the car into the median, hoping to keep us out of the path of the big trucks. I offered a silent prayer to G-d. Or maybe it wasn't silent. What in the world should we do?

At just that moment a car whizzed past us and then screeched to a stop in front of us, backed up, and came up alongside us. And would you believe? It was a mechanic — and not just any mechanic, but a Jewish mechanic! He said he had seen the yarmulkes on my husband's and son's heads, and figured they didn't know much about cars – a fair assumption, I might add – and decided to stop and see if he could help.

He opened the hood, tinkered for a few minutes and worked his own form of mechanical miracle. Within ten minutes our recalcitrant car roared to life. Thank G-d! And thanks to a professional Jewish mechanic who stopped to help a brother in need.

All the way home, we were talking and laughing about our miracle mechanic, but the kids had another idea: it was Elijah the Prophet, they said, disguised as a mechanic, who really came to our aid.

On Spirit

Very Holy People Can Point The Way

The previous stories were of "coincidences," those little – or not so little – things which demonstrate to us that G-d is looking out for our best interests, always, in everything. Sometimes He uses the juxtaposition of things – names, lost items, missed events, even the misplaced devotion toward hunks of stone and wood – to remind each of us of His constant care.

Yet "coincidences" aren't the only ways G-d has of demonstrating His presence. He also utilizes very holy people right here on Earth to actually, physically, point the way for us. *Tanach* (a Hebrew acronym for *Torah, Nevi'im, Kesuvim,* or

Torah, Prophets and Scriptures) is filled with stories about such special people: our father Abraham, who defied his father's idols and came to know G-d by studying the heavens, spreading knowledge of the one G-d everywhere he went; Moses, who communicated with G-d and recorded the Divine Will and Wisdom into the Torah, our guidebook, that is the basis for our lives today; Aaron the High Priest, and Miriam the Prophetess who guided our way in the desert. Thousands of specially gifted people, from the prophets who told G-d's Word to the people, to great men like King David and King Solomon who led us by G-d's hand, and heroes like Esther and Mordechai who saved us from certain death. And there are many more.

But it isn't only in Biblical times that G-d used gifted, specially chosen people to show us the way. Great Sages like Rabbi Akiva spoke G-d's Word and showed us how to live. Later, brilliant men like Rashi and Maimonides interpreted those words and wrote them down for us, in a form we understand and live by today.

And even today, in our own time, G-d uses holy and wise people to point the way. The history of the Chassidic movement tells this story better than almost anything else. Let me take a minute to tell you where we Chassidim (plural of Chassid) came from, and who the people were who brought us to this point.

The Rise Of The Chassidic Master

By the late sevententh century, world Jewry was at a low ebb. Not only were Jews devastated by the incessant pogroms they faced, but we were sharply divided within our ranks. Although a small percentage of Jews were supremely well-educated, enjoying the best Torah education our people have ever enjoyed – offered through a system of remarkable Jewish schools for boys and young men – the vast majority of individual Jews had hardly any education at all. Lacking funds to pay for a formal education of any kind, they struggled to learn the simplest daily prayers from their fathers. Making this dismal state of affairs worse was the fact that there seemed to be no hope for the chronically impoverished. How could they improve their lot with no education? And with no education, their commitment to Judaism seemed likely to wither on the vine.

What made the system even more unfortunate was that the well-educated Jews tended to look down on their simple brethren — a still-common part of human nature, perhaps. But the Jews who were educated were too few to assure the continuation of the Jewish people — after all, it was the well-educated and better-off Jews who were the frequent targets of hostile non-Jewish neighbors looking for easy wealth. In short, the Jewish world seemed on the brink of destruction.

It was at this point that G-d took pity on His people and sent a tremendous leader and charismatic wonder-worker to reinvigorate Jewish life. The man – Rabbi Yisrael (Israel) – was known simply as the Baal Shem Tov (1698-1760), the "Master of the Good Name." When someone faints and you whisper their name in their ear, they revive. The House of Israel, the Jewish people, was spiritually fainting. So the Jews' collective name, *Yisrael,* was "whispered" to them in the form of Rabbi Yisrael; the Baal Shem Tov's arrival and revival.

It was the Baal Shem Tov who undertook a lifelong role to raise Jewish spirits, even that of the poorest, least educated Jew. Traveling the Eastern European countryside, the Baal Shem Tov taught poor, dispossessed, disheartened Jews that true religion consisted not only of scholarship, but also of a sincere love of G-d combined with warm faith and belief in the power of prayer. He counseled that the ordinary person filled with a sincere belief in God, and whose prayers come from the heart, is more acceptable to God than someone versed in and fully observant of Jewish law who lacks inspiration in his learning and performance of mitzvahs.

To these suffering Jews, nearly broken by poverty, persecution and alienation, the words of the Baal Shem Tov offered hope, joy, inspiration and even life itself. The Baal Shem Tov's message of G-d's unconditional love for each of His chosen people, regardless of their level of learning or circumstances, spread across the bleak European continent like wildfire, igniting every Jewish soul it touched, bringing the warmth and love of G-d to a whole world of Jewish hearts that had nearly frozen in despair.

The Baal Shem Tov was famous for his stories and parables, which contained both easily graspable insights, for the laymen, and profound depth, for the great scholars. By oral transmission these sayings spread like wildfire across the countryside. With beautiful tales of simple Jews – and women who stood by their men, struggling shoulder to shoulder to raise families and nurture faith – the Baal Shem Tov showed the masses the way to a life of perfect Jewish observance and wholesomeness, all amplified with sheer joy.

When at last, at the age of sixty-two (very old for those times), the Baal Shem Tov returned his loving soul to G-d, he was succeeded by a man almost as remarkable as he had been, although with talents of a very different nature.

Rabbi Dov Ber of Mezritch (1704-1772), a man who was, in many ways, the mirror image of the Baal Shem Tov, took over as leader of the rapidly growing movement known as *Chassidism* (the pious ones). Named by their early opponents, it is a term traditionally used by the rabbis to describe those Jews who maintained the highest standard of religious observance and moral action. Rabbi Dov Ber – called "the *Maggid*" (the Preacher) – was a powerful teacher, as well as a consummate organizer and writer. He set about establishing order among the legions of the Baal Shem Tov's devoted followers, writing down key elements of his teachings and organizing other leaders to take the message out to the farthest reaches of the Jewish Diaspora. The Baal Shem Tov was the spark that ignited

Jewish souls across the world, but it was the Maggid's organization and foresight that fanned the flames and kept the fledgling Chassidic movement alive and growing.

The Maggid had hundreds of successors. His students spread out across Europe, spreading the Baal Shem Tov's message of hope and service of G-d with love and joy. Each of them formed, with his own followers, a distinct type of Chassidism. Rabbi Schneur Zalman of Liadi, "the *Alter Rebbe*" (the Elder Rebbe), as he came to be called after his passing, was the main successor to the Maggid.

The Alter Rebbe (1745-1813) was the founder of Chabad Chassidism, or Chabad-Lubavitch, Lubavitch being the name of a town in White Russia that served as the sect's base of operations for many years. Of note, the word "Lubavitch" means "city of love." The Alter Rebbe was a consummate philosopher and a prolific author, writing several commentaries on law and observance, including a compilation of Chassidic teachings called the *Tanya* — a classic philosophical treatise on morality and human behavior that intimately addresses the permanent, ongoing struggle within the self, and is still studied the world over.

In line of succession, there have been six more Chabad Rebbes since the Alter Rebbe, the seventh having been my spiritual guide, the Rebbe, Rabbi Menachem M. Schneerson (1902-1994).

Our Rebbe – a phrase Chabad Chassidim use now to refer

only to Rabbi Menachem M. Schneerson – is, by any standard, one of the most remarkable men of modern times. A Torah prodigy as a young child and a truly righteous person his entire life, he was educated at the University of Berlin and at the Sorbonne before escaping prewar Europe in 1941 just ahead of the Nazis. When his father-in-law (the sixth Chabad Rebbe, Rabbi Yosef Y. Schneersohn, referred to as "the previous Rebbe") passed away in Brooklyn in 1950, Rabbi Schneerson succeeded him as Rebbe.

Before the Holocaust, there were hundreds if not thousands of different Rebbes in Eastern Europe, each leading his own group of followers in a unique branch of Chassidic Judaism. Each group was distinguished by slight differences in custom and tradition, but united in philosophy and observance. After the unspeakable loss of the six million, however, relatively few Chassidic groups managed to survive — only those who, somehow, had already established roots outside of Europe. It was through the remarkable leadership of the previous Rebbe and, mainly, Rabbi Menachem M. Schneerson that Chabad Chassidism replanted itself in Brooklyn and ultimately gained prominence throughout the world.

Someone once asked Rabbi Shalom Dovber (grandfather-in-law of the Rebbe), "What is a Chassid?" And he replied, "A Chassid is a lamplighter."

The lamplighter, as our own grandparents might be able to tell us, was the man who went around town every night to light the gas street lamps with the flame he carried at the end of a long stick. Sometimes the lamps were easily accessible and ready to burst into flame. Others were hard to find — they were in forsaken places or, metaphorically, they were in the desert, or at sea.

The Torah tells us that the soul of every Jew is like a flame. To us in Chabad, it can also be likened to one of those street lamps, ready and waiting to be kindled. Some are near and easy to reach, ready to give light of their own. Others are far off, in hard-to-reach places — in the desert or out at sea. A Chassid is someone who will forgo his or her own comforts and conveniences, and reach out to light all those other lamps.

No one in modern times has lit the waiting wicks of so many Jewish lamps as our Rebbe. In addition to establishing outreach centers, Chabad Houses, all over the world, one of the most remarkable ways the Rebbe reached out to Jewish souls was by way of Dollars — standing for hours every Sunday afternoon, handing out a dollar for charity to anyone who wanted one, together with a blessing and perhaps a word of encouragement.

We've already talked about the hows and whys of Dollars (see *With Sensitivity to All*, above), and now it's time to look at some of the results. Perhaps some of the stories of people who came for Dollars will do more to explain why the Rebbe did it than anything else I can write.

Esther's Wedding

This story happened after I had been teaching "my brides" for several years, plus running a Hebrew school for children and teaching older girls in preparation for their bat mitzvahs. Life was full and exciting. Thank G-d, many Hebrew-school children were being drawn to Judaism, but that was not always something that delighted their parents. At one particular time, I was dealing with people in my community who thought a little Jewishness might be okay in the abstract, but when it came down to their lifestyle – where (and what!) they could eat, and driving on Shabbat – it became understandably threatening. This feeling that I was getting on the parents' nerves with my religion bit had been carrying on for several months, throughout which I faithfully went to weekly Dollars to get blessings from the Rebbe for myself and for my activities, the stresses of which the Rebbe knew very well. It was only because of the Rebbe's ongoing encouragement that I was able to continue at all.

On this particular day in 1992, however, my teaching did not come up at all. I stood in line at Dollars, and when I got to the front I received a dazzling smile from the Rebbe. He handed me my usual dollar for myself and one for my husband. And then, a complete surprise: he gave me one more dollar "for your daughter Esther's wedding!" The Rebbe's smile was the biggest I'd ever seen!

The only thing was that my daughter Esther, then twenty-one, wasn't getting married at that time if she could help it.

As I started to walk away, everyone who had overheard what the Rebbe said started saying "Mazel tov!" to me, wishing me – and my daughter! – happiness. I was stunned. I was even more stunned when moments later, the Rebbe called me back and handed me another dollar, this one "for your other daughter's wedding, which will follow soon after Esther's!" Daniella, my youngest, was nineteen then. Again, that big grin.

This was almost too much — my daughter Esther wasn't a bride, and my other daughter was certainly not getting married anytime soon, either. But the Rebbe didn't make that kind of mistake — and he clearly hadn't mistaken me for someone else. He *had* asked about my husband's trip, and he had mentioned Esther by name, had he not? All I could think was: "What?!"

But in due time, the mystery was cleared up. It was only a short time after this Dollars that the Rebbe had a stroke and was bedridden. He knew he would not be there to give my daughters dollars as their weddings approached. And indeed, within two years, both Esther and Daniella were happily married.

That was the Rebbe's way: always thinking about other people and their needs, never his own. Since the times of the Baal Shem Tov, Chassidic Rebbes have been known for having certain powers — knowing things that people don't, for example. There are many stories of this type about our Rebbe. This one staggered even me.

The Trip To Israel

One year, in November, I had to make an emergency trip to Israel to visit my parents in the city of Bat Yam. My father had become very ill and was asking for me. I did as I always did — I made travel arrangements and then wrote to the Rebbe, telling him my plans and asking for his blessing for a safe journey. To my surprise, I didn't receive an answer; the Rebbe didn't even send me *shliach mitzvah* money. (The Torah teaches that someone in the process of performing a mitzvah will come to no harm, as he is protected by the holy activity. When followers of the Rebbe would travel, the Rebbe would give them *"shliach mitzvah"* money — a small sum of cash. The person then became the Rebbe's *shliach,* agent, to deliver this money to a charity in the foreign country, and thus would be granted a safe journey by way of being a mitzvah agent.) But this time I received no such blessing — and no shekels for delivery to charity in Israel!

The situation soon resolved itself. I developed an unpleasant flu and had to postpone my trip. And just as I was recovering, my husband's family arrived from Milan, Italy, to spend three weeks with us, thus postponing my trip again.

After everyone left, I remade my plans and wrote to the Rebbe I was now really going to Israel. He responded immediately with a blessing for my father's restored good health and ten shekels, one for each day I would be in Israel. (How did he know I was going to be in Israel for ten days? I never told him.)

My father did recover, thank G-d, and by then I understood why the Rebbe hadn't sent the shekels the first time! He knew I wasn't going just then.

Just In Time

There was an Iranian lady in our community named Esther, with a son named Michael. Was this Esther ever a skeptic! She'd hear stories about the Rebbe, but would always laugh and shake her head. "How can people believe that stuff?" she would snicker, always able to offer another "perfectly simple" explanation for what had happened.

But Esther's son Michael was a bit of a problem — well, more than a bit, actually. Some of it was really not his fault. The poor Jews of Iran have had their problems, and Michael was heir to many of them. Since the Islamic Revolution, when so many Iranian Jewish families had to flee for their lives, many family problems developed. Not only were the refugees suddenly in a foreign country – the U.S., in this case – where they didn't speak the language, didn't understand the culture and were suddenly living in abject poverty, but in their immediate past, in Iran, they may have been well-to-do doctors, lawyers and professors. You can imagine the stress they experienced when those credentials did not automatically transfer to American society. All the immigrants would have to take new tests, and all in a new language. And in the meantime, they had to earn their livelihood by the most menial labor they could find. This was a considerable adjustment for many.

Another problem was even worse. In many families, the

Iranian parents had first sent their children out of Iran to assure their safety while they tried to salvage what they could. They hoped to later find a way out themselves. Those young children, without parental guidance in a foreign land, suffered tremendously. What little Jewish education many of them had before they left was soon lost as they all-too-quickly assimilated into the worst parts of American culture. With no Jewish knowledge, no Jewish community, and no parental love or control, they rushed headlong into Western "freedom" — quitting school, using drugs, and worse. Seeing this, the Rebbe organized a rescue team to help many of these alienated Iranian young people.

Michael had been one of those early-on-his-own children, sent off by his well-meaning mother, Esther, who was simply trying to save his life. Michael, in his teens, had been sent directly from Iran to Los Angeles, as were his brother and sister later on. Esther had finally been able to get out and arrived in New York, only to hear that Michael had fallen in love with a non-Jewish girl, a daughter of a German and a Muslim. She pleaded with her faraway son on the phone, as did the brother and sister, but to no avail. Michael simply cut off contact — he changed his phone number and told everyone he would do as he pleased, and to leave him alone.

As you can imagine, the family was devastated. What to do? Michael wasn't a child. Now in his early twenties, he could legally do whatever he wanted. Esther, who had scoffed at the Rebbe's stories, now came to me, sobbing. "Can you ask the Rebbe for help?" she asked. "Maybe a blessing from him?" If Esther was now asking for his help, then she must have been quite desperate.

We went to the very next Dollars and Esther, in tears, begged the Rebbe for help. The Rebbe told us to "expect good news," and Esther received a dollar for Michael. We mailed the dollar to Los Angeles, together with a letter containing the kind of prayers only a mother in such a situation can utter. And then we waited.

It took three weeks, and then Esther took a call from her daughter Yaffa in Los Angeles. She said that the strangest thing had happened. It was only four days before Michael's upcoming wedding – an event they still could not comprehend and had been unable to speak to Michael about for many weeks – when Yaffa was startled by a ferocious banging on her front door. She opened it, and was astonished to see her brother Michael, disheveled, sobbing and completely distraught. "What was I doing?" he cried. "I can't believe I was about to marry that girl!"

If you think about it, in every generation there has been, somewhere in the world, a force separating Jewish children from their heritage. In ancient times, the constant assaults and killings were commonplace. Then the Crusades, followed by the repeated expulsions from country after country until there was almost no place left to go. In more modern times, the Cantonist movement forced Russian Jewish boys, as young as ten, into the army for twenty-five-year terms and took a huge toll in death and loss of identity. Then, the Holocaust. And now, the ravages of assimilation.

In our time, the assault is not over. Even secular historians agree that the Jews, as a people, could never have survived these thousands of years of forces arrayed to wipe us out, if not for some inexplicable counteracting force.

Maybe for them it's "inexplicable." Not for us. We know something they don't — we know who we are.

At times, a Jewish soul can merely be unaware or forget who he or she is. And, at some of these times, a Rebbe might ignite a lost Jewish soul into a roaring self-consciousness that returns it to its roots.

Optimism And Simple Faith

Edna, another Iranian woman in our community, has a fascinating background and many distinguishing characteristics. But when I think of her, I think of her selfless devotion to her son and daughter. Although the family lived in frightful poverty, Edna managed, through means I could never imagine, to send her children to a good Jewish school instead of public school. Edna was always a particular source of inspiration to me — she did so much with so little, with never a complaint.

But one day I had a phone call from Edna that was not inspiring. She was very upset and clearly shaken and afraid. A tumor had been discovered and the biopsy was not good at all, she told me. "What can I do?" I asked, my mind racing even as my heart was breaking. Poor Edna! And who was she worried about, even at this moment? Not about herself but her children. How would they carry on, she wondered, if she were not in the picture?

Through my own tears I asked, "Can I bring you to the Rebbe?" Of course, that was no problem. Sunday we would go for Dollars and ask for a blessing.

On the drive into Brooklyn, I kept telling her about what the Rebbe had told us about that year (Hebrew-calendar year

5751, or 1991): It was to be a year of personal, individual miracles. And the best way to have achieved your miracle was to be happy and to trust in G-d.

Edna was extremely touched by the Rebbe's blessing for a *refuah shleimah* (a restoration of health) and good news, and on the way home relived the experience over and over again in sheer wonder. For me, this was again one of those occasions in which I learned so much from other people. Edna was another one of those young Iranians who had very little Jewish education or knowledge. But in terms of trust? If only we all lived at her strong level of faith!

Her treatment moved ahead and Edna was scheduled for an operation to remove the tumor on the same day I was to leave for Israel. I didn't hear the results until I came back. I was more than a little worried, I can tell you. But one morning the phone rang and there was Edna — cheery, happy and bubbling with joy. *"What happened?"* I asked. By this time, I had to assume the news was good.

"I just listened to the Rebbe," she said. "Remember? He said we should be happy, and to think positive. That was the way to realize our blessings. So I did that, to the best of my ability. I kept my family in high spirits and constantly encouraged everyone to think good thoughts. I decided to thank G-d every day, fifty times! Do you know what happened? [By this time I was ready to burst, wondering what *did* happen!] When I went back to the doctor after seeing the Rebbe, there was no tumor. NO TUMOR. It had disappeared! Not that it had never been there, you understand — they'd biopsied, after all! It had been there, but it had now disappeared!

"You see?" she continued. "The Rebbe was right! This is a year of miracles for my family and me. Not only do I not have a tumor anymore, but you should see what has happened to my children — new life has come into them. They saw how I was handling this, and we talked about what the Rebbe had said, about being happy, thinking positive, living in joy. Somehow it all came together. The wonderful education they are getting in Jewish school, the love, warmth and joy in our home — I am so happy!"

I doubt if any of G-d's miracles has ever been received in greater joy — I feel humble in the presence of such simple, pure faith and trust. You can be sure this was one story I could hardly wait to pass back to the Rebbe!

Blessedly Vanished

Cancer. Surely one of the most horrifying words in the English language. An affliction before which we all feel vulnerable.

In "olden times," people died from so many things: plague, typhoid, cholera. Even smallpox or measles could be lethal, not to mention all the other diseases that could be fatal without any treatment, such as pneumonia. Now those diseases are virtually under complete control. Now we eat healthier and have the blessings of clean water, antibiotics, penicillin and all the wonder drugs (although the holistic "alternative route" works for me). The disease of our generation is cancer. Maybe this is because we live long enough to get it, which wasn't the case in days gone by.

There are many stories of the Rebbe and cancer patients — enough to be recounted in a book of their own. But one in particular may be told here.

I once took a young couple with three little children to Dollars. They were all extremely agitated, as the husband had just been informed he had cancer.

We stood in the Dollars line (my groups had permission

from the Rebbe for direct access) and both the husband and wife struggled to control their emotions. And who could blame them? So much to live for! Such a beautiful family! When their turn came they stepped up to the Rebbe, and the woman could control herself no longer. She burst into wrenching sobs, beyond comfort. "Oh please, G-d," I found myself praying. "Let something good happen here."

"Healing" comes in many forms, of course. There is spiritual healing as well as physical. As tears rolled down my own face, I saw the husband lean forward and whisper to the Rebbe, as though the words themselves could not be spoken aloud, "I have been ill. They found I have cancer."

I don't know what, exactly, I expected from the Rebbe. The beauty of his encouraging smile? A heartfelt blessing, a dollar, a blessing for good health? All of those things would have helped. But I did not expect what followed.

"NO!" the Rebbe shouted. "NO! THEY DID NOT! They did not find cancer!" He waved his arm as if to brush off some unseen lurking evil. He handed several dollars, one at a time, to the shocked couple, each with a strong, positive wish for good news and positive results, and for faith and goodness throughout. But the power of his words was greater than the words themselves. There was so much energy – life-filled energy, power and strength – that the words themselves were dwarfed by the loud authority with which they were spoken.

Indeed, as the Rebbe said, they had not found cancer — at

least not by the time the man went back to the doctors.

Tests were performed and repeated, again and again. There was no explanation — but neither was there any cancer. Finally, the doctors gave the man a clean bill of health — you could sense the state of bewilderment as they walked away. There was no cancer. None at all.

Affliction and healing are in G-d's hands. And in this case, the overriding results were completely positive. But there was more than *one* miracle in this story: the little family – now perfectly intact, thank You, G-d! – is now well on its way to being completely observant.

Losing Everything...

As the years went on, and as my involvement with Chabad and the Rebbe increased, I found myself bringing more and more people to Dollars. It seemed to me that one of the best things I could do for the world at large was to bring as many Jews as possible to the Rebbe, hoping that his infectious faith and his tremendous love of G-d, Torah, mitzvahs, fellow Jews and humanity would rub off on them, inspire them and give them new incentives to live a G-dly and observant lifestyle. For a time, I even hired buses and arranged central pickup spots where people I had invited could meet and travel together to the Rebbe. The buses would be literally packed with people from all over the world, speaking many languages, all joined together to visit one of the holiest men of our times. I can't tell you the pleasure this gave me — and the things I saw, the stories I heard! There were so many personal accounts that came out of these trips, so many miraculous events, so much joy restored, so much peace renewed. You can only imagine how I looked forward to each and every Sunday, when I could give several dozen people their first chance to see and meet the Rebbe, as well as the merit to stand by them, close to the Rebbe, as I would be helping my group pass by!

As you might expect, there were all kinds of people on these buses, not only from all parts of the world, but from all segments of Jewry. Sometimes the newest and most impoverished immigrants would end up sitting next to people who were nationally prominent — wealthy financiers, political officials or Jewish leaders in their own communities.

One particular trip I remember well. Two of the biggest philanthropists in our own community were going to be with us. This couple was very distinguished and prominent in many circles, and, as I learned on the trip, had just suffered a considerable personal loss: their home had just been burglarized. In addition to losing many very valuable antiques and almost priceless rugs, the wife's entire personal collection of jewelry had been taken; a costly monetary loss and a considerable sentimental loss as well. Both husband and wife were very upset and nervous as well, living in fear now that their sense of personal safety had been violated.

But they were delighted to be going to the Rebbe and breaking away from the intense focus on what they had lost. I found it especially interesting that this couple was frequently in the company of dignitaries and heads of state. They would be accustomed, one would think, to being near to centers of power. But as we moved up in the Dollars line, I could see their nervousness — they were apprehensive about meeting the Rebbe! As soon as they stood face-to-face with the Rebbe, I introduced them, and both husband and wife were simply speechless. Neither could say a thing. The Rebbe, in his unassuming, gentle and warm way, smiled at them and gave each a dollar bill and a blessing. He then turned to the wife, gave her an extra dollar, and said, "This is for you, for helping your husband."

They walked out in a daze — they had completely forgotten about their lost possessions! What really bowled them both over was the Rebbe's comment about the wife's help. "How did he know?" she kept asking. Neither of them ever talked about it, but, as it turned out, it was the wife's business acumen that had caused their business to flourish. She was the one who had done the hard work, who possessed the sterling business sense (not to mention the mazel) that put the whole business operation together. This was not something that the rest of the world knew — and until now, no one had ever mentioned it!

You can imagine how important those words of acknowledgement were to the wife — and to the husband too, actually. He valued and needed his wife's assistance and support, but was not in the habit of telling her so very often.

Looking back on that day, what struck me was that on the trip to see the Rebbe, the only topic of conversation was their considerable losses. On the trip back, however, the only topic was their many blessings — including each other, their good health and the many good breaks they'd both had over the years.

...And Gaining Everything

At least once a year I would take the children of my Hebrew School in Queens to see the Rebbe at Dollars. It was so obvious that the Rebbe loved those children. He "micro-managed" each one, taking the time to talk, really talk, to each of them. You could feel the love he felt for them, and they for him.

Our bar mitzvah-class teacher, a young man named Avi, once came with our group as well. He brought his wife along. When she got to the Rebbe, he gave her an extra dollar and said, "Thank you for helping and supporting your husband. Please continue."

When we exited 770 Eastern Parkway (Lubavitch world headquarters), I noticed that Avi's wife was grinning from ear to ear, with a deep blush spreading across her pretty face. Avi, too, was beaming. "What are these two up to?" I thought, knowing that something had happened that had touched them both very deeply. They soon told me.

"Avi's teaching has been taking a lot of time," his wife said, blushing all over again. "I'm embarrassed to admit, I haven't been happy about it. Not only was it taking up his time from our family, but he's losing time from work over it, too. I've wanted him to quit the teaching for a long time, but he didn't want to. I argued he shouldn't have to be teaching those unruly public school kids, but he just couldn't give it up. He felt it was something he did for G-d. But just last week, I said I'd had enough, and Avi finally agreed."

"So this advice came just in time," Avi said. "It would have been a terrible mistake for me to quit — for some of those kids, this is the only Jewish thing in their lives. Most of the parents don't have anything else Jewish in their homes at all. They just send the boys off to bar mitzvah classes. I may not see miracles every day, but who knows? The day may come in future years when something they've learned in our classes will hit home, and they'll remember it."

"And I see it now," said his wife. "I was very wrong to urge him to quit. The Rebbe helped me to see that."

That is how the Rebbe was. We could see how much he loved the children. We knew those kids were going to remember that day as long as they lived, and that they would go home and tell their parents all about it. How could we abandon those kids when a man as busy and important as the Rebbe obviously cared about them so much?

"I have a feeling that I'm teaching the parents, too," Avi said, smiling. "The kids go home to their parents and tell them about Judaism. In a lot of those homes, it's the children who are teaching the parents!" (Indeed, one of the signs of the coming of Moshiach is described by the verse, "And he will turn the hearts of fathers toward sons, and the hearts of sons toward their fathers.")

"And we're not quitting," Avi's wife added.

And they didn't. The power of appreciation made all the difference.

Acts Of Kindness

David, a member of my husband's family and a staunch agnostic, was suffering from complete kidney failure and had been on dialysis for some time. Finally, we all rejoiced when a kidney for transplant became available. At last, we thought, some hope.

David had the operation, but in the days that followed, it became apparent that he was not doing well. His body was rejecting the kidney. The doctors tried everything, every treatment and the full range of chemicals, but nothing was working and they were growing pessimistic about his chances for survival. As his teenaged children (the youngest was fifteen at the time) waited in another room, the doctors had to explain to his wife what serious trouble David was in.

A few days later I had a call from a mutual friend: They had now been advised there was little hope at all. He could go at any time.

It was a Sunday, the day the Rebbe gave out dollars, and I was shocked: Someone was calling to say *there was no hope?* No way! I hopped in my car and drove at something beyond the speed limit all the way to 770 where the Rebbe still stood, giving out dollars. (This was an emergency, after all. I would have welcomed a police escort!) When I faced the Rebbe, I told him

— On Spirit —

the name, loud and clear: David son of Sarah. I asked for a blessing of *refuah shleimah*. The Rebbe responded with a dollar for me, a dollar for David and a third one "for your activities and your group," as well as a blessing for David. I can still hear the Rebbe simply saying, *"Refuah shleimah."* I ran back to the car, raced to the hospital, and delivered the dollar.

Now let's talk about hope! You can guess: David's condition changed rapidly at about that time. Quite suddenly and unexpectedly, his body accepted the new kidney and he survived. You are free to assume the doctors had finally stumbled on an anti-rejection drug that worked, or …

After it was all over and David was well, I had to ask: "What was going on in your mind? You're an agnostic — or at least you call yourself that. When you were so sick, what were you thinking?"

I wasn't surprised by the answer. I had given David some of Rabbi Manis Friedman's audio tapes. I'm not even sure what the subject of the tapes was, but I knew that audio tapes are ideal for hospitalized patients. In addition to giving the patient something positive piped directly into their brains, they also filter out hospital background noise, which can be considerably detrimental in and of itself. David told me he had been listening to the Rabbi Friedman tapes, and ever so slowly he had begun to realize that he had been wrong. There was a loving Creator, he said. And he had started to believe. In his own way he had prayed, and it had given him strength and hope. (Since his recovery, David and his wife have become ardent admirers of the Rebbe — hardly a surprising result.)

But wait. The story isn't over. Several years later David was again in the hospital, this time for a hip replacement, probably necessitated by the large amounts of chemicals he had been given during those years in which he had suffered from malfunctioning kidneys. This time David was in Mount Sinai Hospital in Manhattan, "coincidentally" at the same time the Rebbe was undergoing a gall bladder operation. And it was at the same time as the traditional seven days of post-wedding rejoicing after the wedding of one of Rabbi Friedman's sons, which was being held in the hospital because of the Rebbe's presence there. They hoped to bring some joy to the Rebbe and the Chassidim by holding the celebration in a part of the lobby reserved at that time for Lubavitcher Chassidim paying a visit to the Rebbe.

I saw this unusual trifecta and realized the connection. There was David, whose life had been saved, the Rebbe, who had interceded on David's behalf, and the rabbi whose tapes had ultimately brought David around. I went to Rabbi Friedman, reminded him of the story and told him that David was upstairs recovering from surgery. Without hesitating a second, Rabbi Friedman gathered up a huge plate of food, left his own celebration and went upstairs to visit David.

Now, picture the scene. There is the stoic David, the former agnostic, in the hospital bed, weak and exhausted from the newest surgery. In the door comes Rabbi Friedman, loaded with food and good cheer, fresh from his own celebration.

David realized at once what Rabbi Friedman had just done, and it was simply too much for him. My no-nonsense, all-business, very dear relative David broke into uncontrollable sobs, simply unable to respond to such kindness — and, as he pointed out, it was a repeated kindness. It was Rabbi Friedman's tapes, he reminded us all, which had given him the strength and courage to survive the first time. And here was Rabbi Friedman again, in person, leaving his own celebration to bring David food — not just food for his starving soul, as he had delivered the first time.

Seeing that kind of selflessness and kindness did the trick. "It was worth more than countless lectures and sermons," David said.

It all fell in place after that. The whole family is now Shabbat-observant. David's son Doron went to Israel to study, and his daughters Sarah and Sharona blossomed into exemplary Jewish girl, modest and refined. And when Sarah ultimately got married, who was the master of ceremonies at her wedding? Rabbi Manis Friedman.

Just The Way You Are

Here's the story of a lovely young girl. Well, she was lovely, but she was in those early-teen years, and in that way young girls have, she didn't always know how lovely she was. Sometimes she thought she was too fat, only to seem far too thin the next day; one day she would hide her face in horror when she saw a spot, and the next day it was her hair that was impossible. All in all, however, our young heroine was both a lovely and a completely normal young girl, who suffered most of the problems of coming of age that were common to her time.

One day, the lovely young girl heard about an outing that one of her Jewish girlfriends was going on — our lovely young heroine was Jewish, you see, but most of her friends were not, which makes it important to tell you that this particular friend was also a Jew.

They were Jews by birth, but that was about where it stopped, there being very little in their homes to remind them of their Jewishness. In our lovely young girl's home, for example, there was only a weathered mezuzah that clung tenaciously to the outer frame of the back door, and a pair of dented and tarnished candlesticks her mother kept on the top shelf of the hall closet, right behind a stack of linen napkins that never saw the light of day, either.

In any event, the upcoming outing was to be a *Jewish* event, a bus trip leaving from her neighborhood in Long Island to go and see the Lubavitcher Rebbe, whom, they said, was a well-known sage and holy man who lived in Crown Heights, a neighborhood in Brooklyn, New York. "Want to come, too?" her friend asked, and somewhat surprisingly, the young girl found herself giving it some serious thought. It wasn't the sort of activity our young girl would usually have chosen to engage in. But it was the summer, and, quite honestly, there wasn't much to do, and she was getting a little bored already. It sounded interesting, and maybe it would be fun. Different, you know? And besides, you never know who you might meet on such a trip.

As she was thinking about it, however, her *mother* – her mother! – also mentioned the bus trip, having heard about it from a neighbor, and said they (her parents and younger sisters) were also thinking about going. That was almost enough to convince the lovely young girl to stay home. Sit on a bus with her kid *sister*?! Really, now. Nevertheless, by that time the excitement all around her was building, until finally she couldn't permit herself to be left out. "Okay," she said, "I'll go."

So the lovely young girl added her name to the bus list, and then began to wonder what, exactly, would happen when they went to the Rebbe's home. Her friends – one of them had been there before – said that the Rebbe was a very old man who somehow managed to stand, for hours on end, handing out dollar bills to everyone who wanted to receive one. The dollar bill was actually a token, she explained. The recipient was supposed to give the dollar to charity. The real thing the people were receiving was the Rebbe's blessing, for "the Rebbe" – and that was all they called him, even those Jews who were less affiliated or observant of their tradition – was supposed to have great insight (or maybe it was foresight) in being able to tell what was going on with someone, even what would later happen to a person. He was also said to have great influence in the heavens, and a blessing from the Rebbe was just about the most powerful help you could really get in terms of having your prayers answered.

Well, this lovely and very modern young girl really didn't quite believe that part. I mean, if G-d wanted to answer your prayers, He could certainly do so if He wished, couldn't He? It wasn't as though He needed someone here on Earth – let alone someone in Brooklyn! – to give Him suggestions! But all the same, as the days passed, the excitement and the stories about the Rebbe grew and took hold in the young girl's mind. Lots of people seemed to know someone, who knew someone else, who had a cousin or an aunt who had talked with the Rebbe and had great things happen as a result. As skeptical as the lovely young girl was, she began to look forward to the trip — more than she would ever have admitted, if the truth be known.

At last the day came, a Sunday, and a bright sunny one it was, too. The lovely young girl decided to wear her newest outfit, a pair of sleek black pants she was convinced made her look at least five pounds thinner than she was (this was one of her "fat" weeks) and a sleeveless blouse in that color of blue that her friends in her algebra class had said was exactly the color of her eyes. She wanted to wear her best, after all. One never knew whom one might meet.

The bus was packed, and everyone was excited — a few people started to sing, mostly the kind of songs they'd learned at a kids' summer camp, which our lovely young girl had never experienced. Not that it mattered. For reasons the girl couldn't quite explain, she was beginning to feel, well, *happy.* "How could that be?" she wondered idly, with her parents (who'd been fighting all week) sitting just six or seven rows behind her, and her kid sister just a few rows behind them. The bus ride wasn't all that long, but the bus was going too slowly to suit this lovely young girl, and even on a Sunday morning there was traffic. But she had people to talk to — two of her classmates from school and a girl she'd gone to dance class with in third grade.

Finally the bus pulled into an unloading area, just a block from "770," which is what the Rebbe's synagogue was called because it was located at 770 Eastern Parkway. Everyone piled out, excited to get off the bus, but a little shy about what to do or where to go next. Sarah Karmely, the lady who had organized the trip, was giving last-minute instructions, directing everyone to stay in line, to keep together, to move along quickly, and also to be patient since there were hundreds if not thousands of people who had come to see the Rebbe on this fine day. She said it was important for everyone to be respectful of everyone else if the lines were to move as quickly as possible.

"Thousands?" the lovely young girl thought, a little dubious. But as she turned the corner, walking dutifully in line as she'd been told, she actually gasped at the sight before her. No question about it! Thousands of people had gathered, most of them standing in long snaking lines that wound 'round and 'round, this way and that.

There were all kinds of people here, of every race, of every age, from newborn babies in strollers to old people who were probably her great-grandparents' age, sitting in wheelchairs. There were young men dressed like Chassidim – long black coats, black hats, white shirts with no ties, and beards – many of whom were no older than she. There were women in hats, women without hats, women in jeans and sports clothes, and women in dresses of every length and description. There were women in wigs, and women in little doilies that they had donned just for the occasion. There were men in jeans, in sports coats and many more in suits and hats; some wore the infamous black fedora hats, but others wore panama hats or golf caps, and many professed loyalty to some athletic team with baseball caps. Quite a few of the men just wore skullcaps, in every color and design, on their heads.

The lovely young girl – who had rather expected to see only people she would somehow recognize as "Jews" – was surprised. There was, simply stated, no way to categorize these people. They were of all types, of all descriptions, of all ages — and apparently from all over the world, judging from the number of foreign languages the lovely young girl heard. Not that she understood any foreign language, you understand. She'd taken Spanish for a year because a foreign language was required, but other than *"si!"* and *"como?"*, not another word of it had taken up permanent residence in her mind.

The people from her bus milled about. Occasionally someone would recognize a familiar face and warm words of "How are you?" and "I've been thinking of you!" were heard, followed by introductions all around. Mostly, they all just stood about, waiting — and she could see that it was going to be quite a wait. The lines of people waiting to see the Rebbe were long, although curiously enough, there didn't seem to be anyone who was impatient. When the lovely young girl thought about what would happen if these kinds of lines ever appeared at the grocery store or the gas station, she had to laugh. "They'd surely trample each other," she thought, and somehow that fact made her more curious yet.

This was, you should know, precisely the sort of situation that would normally have bored the lovely young girl out of her mind: Nothing to do but stand around and wait — and wait for what? To get one dollar from an old man she'd never met? "What I should be thinking," she told herself, "is what am I doing here, anyway? Let me get another bus and go home! At least I'd have the house to myself!" Yet somehow, even as she thought she should have it, the lovely young girl had no desire to leave — even though her mother and father were standing just a few feet away, and her kid sister was right around here somewhere. In looking back on the situation later, trying to understand it, the lovely young girl thought perhaps it was just the novelty of the thing. After all, there was almost a United Nations spread out before her. And they were all standing respectfully in line, talking quietly among themselves, some of them singing, some just patiently watching the elderly man standing on a little platform, way out there in front of them, but getting noticeably closer all the time.

She found herself studying him, the Rebbe, the charismatic gentleman standing next to a kind of lectern, leaning over it to hand out dollar after dollar to each person who paused in front of him. He was not a particularly large man, but there was something about him … she could see that, even from this distance. He wore a plain black coat with an unremarkable black hat, not too big or too small. He had a full, bushy white beard that sort of split in the middle, the way some long beards seem to do, and he probably wore side curls, although the lovely young girl couldn't see them clearly from where she stood. She could barely see his eyes, but she did watch the effect this powerful man was having on the people who accepted the dollar bills he extended toward them. She didn't quite understand how this elderly man could look powerful, even as she acknowledged that he did.

She could see the line of recipients only from the back, of course, but she could tell that many of them broke into tears, or put their hands over their faces. But not out of sadness, she could tell. It seemed to be more, well, more like *joy*. Could that be it? What could he possibly be saying to each of them that would have so powerful an effect? He didn't know all these people, did he? Of course not — none of the passengers on her bus actually *knew* the Rebbe, although some had been here before, for "Dollars," as this was called.

As the lovely young girl watched one person after another approach the Rebbe, listen intently for a moment, maybe nod "yes" or "no," or speak a few words, listen again, and then reach out for the dollar bill the Rebbe extended in his very white hand, she became more and more transfixed. Something was happening here, something the lovely young girl didn't understand at all, but something that was terribly attractive, even magnetic, all the same. At one point, when she had been standing and moving forward so slowly for almost two hours, she laughed to herself when she realized there was nothing in the world that would make her leave this line — even though she really wasn't quite sure why she was there, or even what she expected to gain from this experience. It was so, well, *holy.*

Could she use that word? She hardly knew what it meant. But some combination of circumstance — the respectful attitude that prevailed, the joy that seemed to bubble up from the people who had just spoken with the Rebbe, the awe that seemed to emanate from just about everyone toward this very powerful man, who seemed to *radiate* goodness, love and respect to every person he handed a dollar to — well, "holy" was the only word she had to describe such a situation, and it would have to fit.

Unfortunately – maybe it was unfortunate, or perhaps it was a blessing – this mood of unparalleled serenity was not to last much longer, not for our lovely young heroine. In fact, when she had come within about fifty feet of the Rebbe, she began to have serious misgivings — not about the remarkable qualities of the Rebbe, who became only more impressive the closer she came, but rather about herself.

She had worn her "best" outfit today: the pants were almost new, and the sleeveless blouse flattered her eyes. But the clothes were, for reasons the lovely young girl could not put into words, *wrong*. The outfit was just wrong. It was too bare on top, and the pants were too tight — not that they were even tight, exactly. Just, the whole thing was not right, entirely the wrong things to have put on at all — not that she could have known that, of course. It was her best. Besides, many people in the crowd were dressed just like her. How wrong could it be? Nevertheless, the first feelings of panic, that iciness in the stomach, the queasy feeling that goes in waves up to your heart, where it clenches so tight you have to force yourself to breathe, took over.

What would she do? Here she was, trapped in pants and a sleeveless top, and there stood the holiest man she had ever seen, had ever *imagined*, for that matter. It was *wrong* — what was wrong? Well, to make this holy man have to look at her, that's what, she decided. It was disrespectful, and the last thing she intended to convey was *disrespect!* She felt herself blushing at the very thought of having to see him, up close. How could she have done this? How could she have been so stupid? Hadn't she known, hadn't she guessed, that arriving in tight pants was so gross a thing to do to such a holy man? She could hardly believe her own stupidity!

The panic increased. She was fifth in line now, and wanted to run away. Looking back, she saw her mother and father behind her, two people back. Like a little girl of three, she ran back to them, shivering in spite of the heat, shaking out of fear of the consequences of what she had done. "How could I do such a thing?" was the question that raced blindly through her mind.

"How could I? How could I?" There had to be a way out.

She could see on her father's face that he didn't understand what was happening. After all, she looked just the way she always looked, and she had never been uncomfortable about it before. She tried whispering to him, but he shushed her, fixing his undivided attention on the Rebbe, who was now just three people ahead. She tried to say she was leaving, going back to the bus – please, please, let me go! – but her father grabbed her hand and held her fast. She had no choice. She couldn't run now. They were next. So she did the best she could. She stepped behind her father, who stood next to her mother (for once), and she hid. Yes, she hid. She cowered behind her parents, and prayed, actually *prayed,* that the Rebbe wouldn't see her. "Oh, please, G-d, don't let him see me! I didn't know. I'm sorry, so sorry! Please, G-d, let me get by him without having him see me like this!"

All prayers are answered, of course, and this fervent one was, too — it was, after all, perhaps the first real prayer our lovely young heroine had ever uttered. But G-d, in that way He has, answered in quite a different way than she – or we – might have expected. The lovely young girl's father stood in front of the Rebbe, accepted the dollar, and then there was silence, total silence, a stillness that enveloped the whole world. It had to, for nothing but the girl cowering behind her father and the Rebbe existed just then. And the Rebbe was not only seeing her, he was seeking her out. He was talking quietly, in words she neither heard or remembered, but he was looking for her, seeking her out, wherever she was, coaxing, pleading. He reached out his hand with the dollar but it was only his eyes that she saw: The most piercing, loving, all-seeing eyes she had ever seen. And the eyes were laughing, too, in the sheer delight of having found her, though she was hiding there, afraid.

Instinctively, the lovely young girl put out her hand to take the dollar, and at that moment, his eyes locked on hers, and in that timeless instant, the world changed, forever. There was no judgment in those eyes, no criticism, no embarrassment. All those laughing eyes conveyed was love, and acceptance, and joy, bubbling over into a gentle laughter at this strange situation in which he, the Rebbe, and she, the lovely young girl, found themselves, in which, for an instant, they were the only two people in the world.

This is not, as you might guess, the end of the story. Rather, it is the beginning. Many things changed for the lovely young girl after that day on which she met the Rebbe as she hid there, behind her father, dressed in her new black pants and a blue sleeveless blouse.

But all that will have to be told later — maybe one day the lovely young girl will tell it herself. Watch for it — our lovely young girl now goes by her Hebrew name, Shaina; perfect for someone as lovely as she. And her children – her two girls in long dresses, her three boys in fringes and yarmulkes – are told the story, the one about the first time their beautiful mother met the Rebbe, many years ago, when she was very young, and very lovely, indeed.

On Commitment

Sometimes G-d Has To Get Our Attention

Sometimes G-d chooses to use another person to point the way, but sometimes He is more direct. Occasionally, He uses events in our lives to get our attention — maybe with illness, as He did in my husband's case. But sometimes all it takes is a gentle nudge.

All of us suffer from disappointments, times when things don't seem to be going well, or periods in which we feel dissatisfied with no obvious cause. When these happen, it's a good time to look around and take stock: are there changes needed? That's why these "disappointments" are usually blessings in disguise. They are G-d's way of pointing us in directions of greater opportunity.

One such incident was a uniquely frustrating trip I took —
one of those in which everything seemed to be going wrong. The
Torah advises a Jew not to begin a trip on a Friday because
things can happen, delays can occur, and you might not get
home (or to your destination) before Shabbat arrives. I knew
that, of course. But I had to travel. Worse yet was that I had to
make this trip during the Nine Days, the period of semi-mourn-
ing in remembrance of the destroyed temple in Jerusalem that
occurs during the first nine days of the Hebrew month of Av.
During those days we don't eat meat or drink wine, we don't
wear new clothing, and in general, we prepare ourselves for the
saddest day of the Jewish year, the ninth of Av, Tishah B'Av, a
fast day that commemorates a series of tragic events in Jewish
history. Traveling would normally be off-limits to me during
that period, but I was in Bangkok and had been advised that I
was urgently needed at home. I found travel arrangements that
seemed as though they would work: Thailand is exactly on the
other side of the world from New York, a full twelve hours
ahead, and so I would travel westward, avoiding the
International Date Line and thus staying one step ahead of the
sunset and the arrival of Shabbat as I flew. Because of the
resulting time zone changes, my proposed itinerary showed that
although I was to leave Bangkok Friday morning, I would reach
New York at least four hours before Shabbat. I booked the
flight and made arrangements to leave Bangkok at 4:30 a.m.
Friday morning. I was solemnly assured by my husband that I
would arrive home in time for Shabbat.

The good news was that I had an excellent traveling companion: Elly, a very successful Iranian Jewish jewelry merchant. I told him I was very nervous about arriving in New York in time for Shabbat. He assured me that he had made this same trip on numerous occasions, and he had never once been late. That helped. I relaxed a little.

We started the trip with a ten-hour flight to Tokyo, which went fine. No problem. There we had a few hours of waiting before the fourteen-hour flight to New York. As we passed the time waiting to board, Elly and I had a chance to talk. He was Jewish but not yet observant, so he was borderline incredulous when I told him that if we arrived in New York after Shabbat began, I would either wait at the airport until the next evening or walk home. I would not take a cab because that would be desecrating the Shabbat. The dedication captured his curiosity, and he began showing interest in learning about his own heritage. He asked many questions about Shabbat and about Judaism in general.

Finally, we boarded the plane to New York — and then we sat. The plane simply didn't take off. It stayed rooted to the tarmac. We sat some more, and still more. As time passed, and as the airline crew seemed to be making no preparations at all, I was becoming increasingly nervous, and it must have worn off on Elly. He started running back and forth to talk to anyone who might have news, explaining that there was a lady on board whom absolutely had to be back in New York by sunset. "When are we leaving?" he kept asking. Finally, two hours late, we took off, and, thank G-d, landed in New York with two hours to spare. Wonderful. But I still had to go through immigration, baggage claim and customs. I don't need to tell you there are times when those little extras can take more than two hours — way more! But now that I was this close, I felt that nothing was going to stop me!

I boarded the shuttle bus that would take us from the plane to the terminal and told the driver, as I went by, that I was a Shabbat-observer, and that I must get through immigration as quickly as possible or I wouldn't be home by sunset. As I was saying this, an American lady in shorts who was standing in line just behind me tugged on her husband's sleeve and said, quite loudly, "Irving, can you believe this? This lady is actually a Shabbat observer!" The whole line of people behind me craned their necks to look. What an oddity! But then she came up to me and said, "I'm Jewish too, but not religious — but you'll see! G-d will help you because you keep the mitzvahs!" I was more than happy for any reassurance.

The shuttle driver, who had now become interested in this strange creature he had on his bus, offered to help. He would show me an elevator with a shortcut, so I would get ahead of everyone — and just to be nice, he told my new Jewish friends they could go with me too, if they wanted. They did.

I finally felt some optimism when I got through immigration without any delay at all, and rushed over to baggage claim to get my bags. But I was too optimistic too soon — I no sooner got over to the claim area when I heard a public announcement: "Due to a mechanical failure, there will be a major delay in baggage pickup."

If I was dismayed, Elly was worse. He had again taken on himself the task of running interference for the lady who guarded the Shabbat. He ran back and forth from one airline employee to another, heatedly lodging complaints when it seemed that might work, offering bribes when that seemed helpful. He told them he would pay whatever it would cost, but "that woman over there" had to have her bags immediately so she could leave for home. It was all to no avail. Nothing could be done. I would have to leave my bags and hop in a cab — I knew my family would be furious if I tried to walk home on the highway in the dark. Plus, I couldn't stay at a hotel: the fast of Tishah B'Av started right after Shabbat, and there was no kosher food. I couldn't fast for two days. I offered a silent, heartfelt prayer to G-d: "Please! All I'm trying to do is follow Your laws! Help me!"

Then, right at that moment, the miracle occurred: there was a rumble and the conveyor belt started to move, and out came my four bags, one after the other!

I was almost struck dumb. But it wasn't over yet since I had done some shopping in Bangkok and I had to go through customs. My purchases were over the amount that was permitted without having to declare anything. With the goal now in sight, Elly piled my bags on a cart he had gotten for me and off we went. He was running, yelling at me to hurry, hurry, hurry. I had no problem with that. The line at customs wasn't huge, but as I waited there, I remembered the last time I went through. It had taken over an hour, as the officer went through every bag, every pouch, every container, looking at every items new and old, asking for receipts. I was psyching myself out. I tried another prayer, this one for serenity.

I got to the head of the line, and the officer started asking questions. My heart sank! As soon as I told him my husband's business was importing gems, he started to get suspicious. I have no idea why. It is perfectly legal, obviously. He dug a little, poked a little, and then asked, "Do you have any food with you?"

Now that's an interesting question. I always take kosher food with me, and I always leave whatever remains for my Jewish friends in Bangkok. But this time, fearing I was going to get stuck somewhere on the journey, I had taken some of it along. It is, of course, illegal to bring food into the U.S. — except for kosher food, although I didn't find that out until months later.

So I started my explanation: "Yes, I have some kosher food. See, I'm Jewish, and the food we eat has to be ... " I went on, digging in my bags and coming up with some items, intending to show him that all the food I had had come from New York, and that I'd bought it here and had taken it with me to Bangkok. It was round-trip American food.

But he held out his hand to silence me, right there, and started digging in his shirt. Up he came with a huge Chai medal that he had around his neck. "See?" he said, proudly. "I'm Jewish too! You don't need to explain kosher to me!" By now he was grinning. My next new friend.

But I was still late – horribly late – and I wasn't especially amused. "If you are Jewish," I began, "then help me get home for Shabbat! I'm Shabbat-observant and if I don't start for home in the next few minutes, I'm going to have to walk all the way to Queens!"

So he started to argue with me. "Well, that's nice for you! What about me?" He was really getting into it. That Jewish soul — get it going, and it never quits! "I have to come in to work tomorrow at 6 a.m.! What am I supposed to do, tell 'em I can't work on Saturday? HA! That'd be interesting! Nice for some people not to work, but what about people like me?"

Oh, he was into it, big time. At this point I started into a lecture about free choice, about the work available for Shabbat observers, about how G-d always helps. Finally I came to my senses and realized what I was doing: arguing when I should be on my way!

I decided to just make a run for it. I picked up two of my bags and ran, leaving my other bags – some opened, some closed – behind. I found a taxi (another miracle!). But here's the biggest miracle of all: the bags I'd left began to show up, one by one, retrieved by the nice people behind me who had heard, and been interested.

With everything in the taxi, I promised the driver a nice tip if he'd get me home fast. He did. Ten minutes to spare. After a while, when I'd had a chance to think about it, I realized that all the frustration and stress had been worth it. It was, of course, all due to Divine Providence. By this time, it was obvious to me that several good things had come out of my frustration. For one, Elly no longer travels on Shabbat or Jewish holidays. And all the other people — who knows? Like the couple in line, Irving and his wife. Maybe seeing someone who is "actually" a Shabbat-observer put a thought in their minds, too. The customs officer? We didn't have time to finish the argument, but maybe he rethought his "need" to work on Shabbat, too. Sometimes these things have to lay inert in our brains for awhile before they take hold.

All in all, it was quite a trip. But very worthwhile!

"Who Is Devorah Leah?"

The story of a lady I will call Yehudit is almost supernatural.

She had been raised in an Orthodox home. Once on her own, however, her exquisite looks, bright, inquiring mind and pleasant nature led her away from Judaism — and not just a little ways away. She lived in utter opulence, but in a manner characterized by crass materialism. Her soul struggled.

When she was still a young woman, Yehudit was diagnosed with a very serious illness, one that would eventually be totally debilitating and for which there was no cure. Her disease progressed more rapidly than was the norm, and she began to panic as she got worse by the day. Someone suggested she contact the Chabad *shliach* in her area. Although she had never heard of Chabad before, nor had any idea what a *"shliach"* was – or even who "the Rebbe" was that he might be an agent for – Yehudit was at the stage where she was more than willing to grasp at straws.

She found her local Chabad rabbi and arranged a meeting, at which he convinced her that the best thing to do would be to fly to New York to visit the Ohel, the Rebbe's grave site. Many wonderful things have happened to people who had enough faith to do that, and the rabbi insisted that this would be good for her.

The term Ohel means "tent" and refers to the structure built over the resting place of a righteous person. On 3 Tammuz, 5754 (June 12, 1994), the Rebbe was laid to rest next to his father-in-law, the sixth Lubavitcher Rebbe, Rabbi Yosef Y. Schneersohn. Our Sages teach that the righteous are accessible and even greater after their passing than during their lifetime, and the Ohel's constant stream of visitors from every sector of the Jewish nation supports their words. It has become a center where thousands come, write letters and notes to the Rebbe and continue to receive inspiration and blessings.

Yehudit's family was outraged. This was foolish, they argued. A superstition. What nonsense! Besides, the long plane ride – which she would have to take by herself, they warned her – would be too stressful. She would be worse when she returned. How could she further endanger herself this way?

She turned a deaf ear to their objections. There was something in her, she said (we'd call it a "Jewish spark," a soul ready to be ignited!) that told her this was the right thing to do. If she had to go by herself, she would. She bought a plane ticket.

The day of departure arrived. She flew without incident, took a cab to the Ohel. While there, a peaceful feeling came over her, but there didn't seem to be any other change. She went home, and after the stress of the day, went to bed and fell sound asleep.

Several days later, she called the Chabad rabbi.

"Who is Devorah Leah?"

"Devorah Leah? Which one? I know several."

"I don't know. *The* Devorah Leah, I guess."

"What's going on?"

"I had a dream the other night. I was in a cemetery, although not that same one where the Rebbe is buried. There was a funeral procession, and as I walked, a very holy-looking woman started walking beside me. 'Who is the funeral for?' I asked. And she told me it was for a person who had died of lupus so that I might live. We walked a little farther, and the woman asked if I would like to go to her father so he could give me a blessing for a complete healing. I said yes. She took me to a very venerable looking man, an older man, who was talking with another man. He interrupted their conversation and gave me a blessing. And just before I woke up, I was told the name of this woman. It was Devorah Leah."

"Well, the Alter Rebbe [see "The Rise of the Chassidic Master," above] had a daughter named Devorah Leah. She sacrificed her life so that her father could live to spread Chassidism so that the Moshiach would come."

"Are … are there any pictures of these people?"

When they next met, the *shliach* opened a book of Chassidic history. "That's him! He's the one who gave me the blessing!"

She was pointing at the picture of the Alter Rebbe.

An incredible story. The Rebbes – all of them, plus their holy families – watch over and help us. The fact that Yehudit was completely cured of her disease is one kind of a miracle.

But there's another interesting miracle here. The fact that Yehudit – sick and weak, discouraged by her family, told that she'd have to make the trip on her own – decided to fly to New York to visit the grave of a man she had never met ... well, that's another pretty remarkable thing, isn't it? There is that spark of Jewishness in all of us that cannot be rooted out, no matter how life or circumstances have treated us — very poorly, in some cases, or lavishly, as in Yehudit's. When it is necessary, when the time comes, that tiny spark and little bit of belief, trust and faith can lead us back to a whole life. And that's what happened to Yehudit.

Today, Yehudit calls herself a Lubavitcher, keeps a "one hundred percent kosher" kitchen, observes the Shabbat and sends all her kids to Chabad schools. Devoted to the Rebbe, a man she never personally met, she now reaches out to others who might not yet have encountered the powerful truth of their Jewish heritage. She is yet another woman of valor that I have been privileged to meet.

In The Light Of The Candle

A couple of years ago I was in Minneapolis at Bais Chana, the Chabad "mini-college" for adult Jewish women's education. One of the women I met there told me another remarkable personal story.

Nancy was one of those people who called herself a "secular Jew" — not observant in any way, but she probably served latkes at Chanukah and bought a box of matzah at Passover in addition to the bag of bagels. In fact, her story starts at Passover, that great celebration commemorating our liberation from slavery to freedom to become the Jewish nation and serve G-d.

One particular Passover, Nancy was vacationing in Florida with her husband when she became sick. When it was apparent that she was indeed very ill, she was rushed to a hospital, where it was determined that all her systems were failing. No one knew why, exactly, but it was obvious she had some sort of infection that was not responding to any treatment. She was about as sick as a person can be and still be said to have a chance.

"I was not at all observant," Nancy told me. "Not in any way. I'd never lit candles for Shabbat, not even once. But as I lay there, so very sick, and more miserable than I can possibly tell you, I felt that I wanted to light candles for the Shabbat. I asked my husband to get some for me – a pretty strange request, I could see in his face. But he did, and even though I was so weak I could hardly strike the match, I lit the candles. I was crying — I didn't even know the blessing. I sank back in my bed and just looked at them. The one candle was burning and melting down in a normal way, but the other ..."

I could see Nancy looking at me, wondering how I would react to this next revelation. "What happened to the other?" I asked, gently, urging her to tell me.

"I saw the Rebbe's face in the flame of the other candle, though I didn't know who he was at the time. I could make out his hat, his face, a beard, and a huge smile. His twinkling eyes winked at me, his head nodding and moving to the flickering light of the candle. I looked and looked, trying to see if it was real, and all that happened was that I felt a wonderful sense of peace. I felt warm, and reassured and loved. It was as if he were telling me, 'It's okay. You will be fine.' I could see his eyes so clearly, blue, looking directly into mine with so much love.

"I must have fallen asleep at some point, although I do remember lying there, looking at the face for sometime. I woke up the next morning feeling fresh and healthy — a complete change from the night before. I insisted on leaving the hospital. The doctors still don't know what happened, but I passed their inspection, so they released me. People kept asking me what had happened, but I couldn't say anything. They would have thought I was nuts!"

"So I decided, right away, that instead of just telling people what had happened, I would show them first. I decided to make up for lost time —to get closer to G-d, to live by His laws, to show the love for others that He had shown to me."

I looked at Nancy now in a new light. Here was this cultured, refined and very intelligent woman, telling me a story that much of the world would find other explanations for: fever, disorientation from drugs, exhaustion, wishful thinking, on and on. But that wasn't how I saw it. It seemed to me that Nancy had been blessed with a private audience with the Rebbe. "The only difference," I told her, "was that he came to you, not the other way around. He came and gave you his help and blessing, what you wanted. Now, return the kindness — show him that his presence and blessing changed your life, that you now keep the mitzvahs. Show him that his effort is really paying off!"

I didn't need to say those things, of course. Nancy, being the highly intelligent and refined woman that she is, had already figured that out.

"He Wants To Hear Their Prayers"

In reading the Torah, one can't help but be struck by the number of women in our family tree who have been barren: Sarah, wife of our Father Abraham, bore her first child at ninety years of age; Rebecca; Rachel; Samson's mother; Hannah, mother of Samuel; the Shunamite woman. All were unable to conceive until their impassioned prayers for children were answered by G-d.

When the question arises, "Why would G-d make all these important women in our family unable to bear children?" the traditional answer is, "Because He wanted to hear their prayers." Obstacles of any kind whatsoever are given to us by G-d because He wants to hear our prayers; He wants to see us strive, grow and elevate ourselves.

I've heard enough stories from women concerning their children, or their inability to conceive, that I can easily see that children, in and of themselves, are still a major inspiration for prayer. Women haven't changed, and neither has G-d. Women are still praying to G-d *for* children and *about* their children, and G-d is still answering — sometimes in ways no one quite expects …

Batya's Baby

Batya and Amos Shiraz are a wonderful couple who have lived in Thailand for many years. Since they were already settled in Bangkok when the Rebbe's *shluchim* first arrived, they were a major source of both inspiration and support in getting the Chabad center up and running.

Batya and Amos had three lovely children and wanted more, but Batya had serious apprehensions. Nothing that she could explain rationally, just a gut feeling that having more children would be a danger to her or to the child. She struggled with this fear for some time, until one day, after a visit to the Rebbe's grave site in New York, that all changed. As she stood there by the grave site, reading her prayerful letter to the Rebbe's soul about her desire for another child, and also her fears, she felt a sensation that he was encouraging her to go ahead. So strong was her sense of his approval that all her fears evaporated and she was overcome with relief and even joy.

Within a short while, Batya conceived again. Even then she was not afraid, although she was nearing forty years of age. "I believe the Rebbe encouraged me. And that means I will be fine," she said. And she meant it. She was very happy.

When Batya was eight months pregnant, I had to travel to Bangkok on business. In due time, everything came to be just as

Batya had believed. We were beyond delighted to hear the wonderful news: Batya had given birth to a healthy, perfect baby girl. Everyone was fine; Batya's intuition had been right.

And then tragedy struck: The day after the birth, Batya suddenly slumped over, put her hands over her ears, shouted, "My head! My head!" and fainted. Within moments she slipped into a deep coma. CAT scans showed the horrible problem — Batya had a suffered a massive hemorrhage in her brain.

Batya's brother, a neurosurgeon who lives in Israel, immediately flew in, as did Batya's sister, who took charge of the four children. Batya had one brain surgery, then another. There were dire predictions. If she lived – a prognosis that seemed in itself doubtful for a time – she would almost surely not regain mobility or memory. With modern technology, of course, they could keep her body alive indefinitely.

After the first horrible shock, Amos never stopped trying to help. He organized prayer sessions for his wife, and then purchased a Torah scroll in her name. Rabbi Yosef Chaim Kantor (executive director of Chabad of Thailand) dedicated hours of vigil in Batya's hospital room. During Rosh Hashanah, he walked miles to and from the hospital to blow the shofar for her. In fact, the whole community responded — the whole Jewish community scattered around the globe. Everyone's heartfelt prayers for Batya rose to the heavens.

And little by little, Batya responded.

She eventually came out of the coma. First, she moved her lips. Then she moved her arms and legs, and then she was able to sit. She walked and eventually talked. Her memory was blurred for a time – she had to be reminded that she now had a new baby girl! – but Batya is now nearly back to normal. I think no mother loves her baby – this one named Esther Malka – and her other children more than Batya does.

"And what of the Rebbe's assurance?" one might ask. "He kept his promise," Batya said. "He did not let us down. I have my baby girl!"

And did G-d get what He wanted? To hear all those prayers from the world over, some from people who perhaps had not been in the habit of talking to Him much before? I dare say yes.

Leave It To Grandma!

One week we had visitors from Milan, Italy — distant relatives of my husband. There were three generations: a set of grandparents, their middle-aged daughter and an adult granddaughter. The latter was a woman who lived in New York and had a very ill husband. He had been diagnosed with lung cancer, and while no definitive prognosis had yet been made, the situation was clearly serious. The purpose of their visit was to seek help from the Rebbe for the ailing son-in-law, husband and father, who was unable to accompany them.

On the ride to 770, everyone was very emotional. In many ways, they believed this was their last chance to find help for the beloved, very sick man. But as they were getting out of the car, the grandmother mentioned that she would also like to ask the Rebbe for a blessing for her own son, a man who lived with his family in Milan. His health was fine, and his family was fine, too, but they had four daughters, and wanted very much to have a son. The grandmother wondered if she would have time to ask the Rebbe for a blessing for her son and his family too. Immediately the other family members jumped at her: No, she was not to ask for her other son! Didn't she understand? The problems with the health of her son-in-law were too serious. Asking for another blessing for something else might somehow "dilute" the power of the blessing for a return to good health for the one who was so ill. Maybe the Rebbe wouldn't take the situation so seriously if something else were also brought up at the same time, they worried.

I could see that the grandmother was a little sad to hear this, but she promised not to mention her son's desire for a son in addition to his lovely daughters.

We waited our turn, slowly making our way to the Rebbe. With a great deal of emotion, the family asked for a blessing for good health for the very sick son-in-law, and the Rebbe responded with his blessing, handing them each a dollar, plus one for the sick man.

And then the Rebbe turned to the grandmother with a huge smile, handed her another dollar and said, "This is for your son, that he should have a baby boy!"

The grandmother burst into fresh tears, and so did we all. The Rebbe *knew* — how could he? How was that possible? We stumbled out in a daze, struggling to come to terms with what we'd heard.

Almost nine months to the day, we heard the news that the son in Italy and his wife were now the proud parents of ... a son.

And lest we forget to mention it, the son-in-law got better. I've been to his family's celebrations many times.

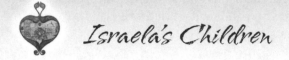

Israela's Children

Israela is a very dear friend of mine, another one of those women from whom, it appears, G-d wanted to hear prayers. She and her husband had been married nine years, but had no children.

For the last five years, Israela and her husband had spent all their extra time – not to mention money, some of which was not exactly "extra" – going from one fertility specialist to another. All to no avail. At this point, even the doctors were suggesting that it was time to consider adoption, while they were still young enough to qualify. In all likelihood, they said, Israela would never bear a child of her own. Even Israela was just about resigned to the fact they would either have to adopt or remain childless.

For some time, I had been suggesting that Israela come with me to seek a blessing from the Rebbe. But to Israela, being so locked up in the science of fertility, doing such a simple thing as asking for a blessing seemed too primitive and too easy — even from a man you respect as being holy. Finally, at the point when they had nearly given up, I was able to convince her to come with me. We would go to the Rebbe for Dollars, and she could ask for a blessing for children. Or, I added, if she was really resigned to being childless, she could ask for help and strength in accepting the life G-d had planned for her. We stood in line, watching, and finally our turn came. Israela, with a sad smile, just asked for "a blessing" with no specific purpose.

In response, the Rebbe handed her a dollar and gave her a hearty blessing for *"gezunte kinderlach* — healthy children!"

Israela and her husband were delighted to hear those words. They recommitted themselves to finding a solution to their childlessness. They went to one more fertility doctor, for yet another attempt, and this one worked! After ten years of marriage, a wonderful healthy little Menachem Yehuda entered this world, a blue-eyed miracle if there ever was one. It was the most joyous *brit* (circumcision) I have ever attended. I think the baby was the only one present who wasn't crying!

And Israela knew there would be more children. "The Rebbe said so!" she said confidently. "He gave me a blessing for 'healthy children'! That means there will be more!" A beautiful baby girl came just a few years later.

Have faith, pray, and trust — and create a receptacle to catch the blessings when they rain down after using help from medical science. If we want blessings, we have to help ourselves!

A meeting of souls at my regular Sunday trek to Dollars. Though you can't see the Rebbe's face, his appearance can be deduced from mine as he smiles, speaks and hands me a dollar bill for charity. (Rabbi Leibel Groner, one of the Rebbe's aides, is seen to the left.)

There is a story behind my beret, which the Rebbe normally advised against. I went before the Rebbe in a beret because at that time my husband FORBADE me to wear a wig. The Rebbe knew this and instructed me not to push the issue. Later, we both grew spiritually and I wore a wig regularly, which, of course, is what Judaism is all about. Most days, I get phone calls from people and from shluchim asking for advice on how to handle one spouse becoming observant before the other...which is my story.

— *Photo Section* —

My husband Benjamin and I, taking in the traditional family dance performed at the wedding of one's youngest child. In this case, our daughter Daniella Miriam was the bride. Moments like this make it all worthwhile.

One of my many speaking engagements on marriage, mikvah, relationships and the Rebbe. This is a keynote address at a fundraising dinner for Chabad of Port Washington.

A special family moment as my late father blesses our son, David, at his bar mitzvah. My father's faith and integrity–and my son's–inspire me to this day.

Amidst the lowly decadence, you'll find seeking Jewish souls – which is exactly where and why you'll also find Chabad. Pictured here is Chabad of Bangkok's Hebrew-language sign, beckoning that city's many Israeli itinerants to find their way home.

Rabbi and Mrs. David and Ronit (center) Loloyan, living out a long-ago promise *(see Out of Iran).* Here, I visit them at their California synagogue.

The epic Jewish mission of bringing light to the nations continues today, as my former co-worker, Frances, expressed gratitude for her new-found faith by gracing a Karmely family wedding.

My precious first grandchild, Yael Sarah, and Yocheved, her angelic late mother, are the very picture of happiness here. Yocheved passed on a few months later.

There is always hope and rejuvenation, healing and happiness — something David (father of Yael Sarah) and Chana Devorah found in each other. A second marriage for each is pictured here, with all the innocence and beauty of the first.

Thoughts to Hear with Your Heart – On Jewish Inspiration and Life

On Asking

But How Do I Ask? Is There A Right Way?

Since the very beginning, Jews have gotten themselves into considerable trouble by asking in the wrong way. Remember what happened in the wilderness, when some of us were getting tired of the manna, the food G-d supplied every day, and decided we wanted *meat?* We complained mightily, going so far as to say that our lives had been better in Egypt, where at least we had meat! We complained mightily, going so far as to say that our lives had been better in Egypt, where at least we had meat!

So what did we do? First we demanded that Moses supply the meat, and then we gathered in groups and wept — what a tantrum! Finally, after Moses got disgusted and frustrated with all the demands, he complained bitterly to G-d, and G-d said fine, He would give us meat. All we wanted, and more! "You shall eat it not one day, not two days, not five days, not ten days, and not twenty days. But even for a full month until it comes out your nose and nauseates you, because you have despised the L-rd Who is among you, and you cried before Him, saying, 'Why did we ever leave Egypt?'" (*Numbers* 11:19-20).

And another one of our demands that didn't work out so well still haunts us to this day. In the days of the prophet Samuel, when Samuel had grown old and his sons were incapable of leadership, once again we became dissatisfied. What did we want this time? A king! Not just a judge or a leader — we wanted a king, just like the gentile nations. So a group went to Samuel and said, "Set up for us a king to judge us like all the nations."

Samuel knew this wasn't a good idea, and it was also confirmed by G-d, who said to Samuel, "Listen to the voice of the people, according to all that they will say to you, for they have not rejected you, but they have rejected ME from reigning over them ..." G-d had Samuel warn us about all the things that would happen if we got what we wanted, "a king like the nations": our sons would be conscripted for armies; we would be forced to perform field work and other hard labor; our daughters would be taken for cooks and perfumers; our precious land would be taken away and given to our slaves; and heavy taxes would be imposed. But did we listen?

Unfortunately not. We thought we wanted what the rest of

the world had. A king. We got a king — and all the things G-d had warned us about.

We learn from here that asking for what we think we want might be dangerous.

But, you might ask, doesn't G-d know what is best for us? Therefore, why should we ask at all? Isn't it better and safer to leave the decision-making in His hands? Or perhaps we should ask but there are some special words involved? Maybe there's a right way to ask. (There's obviously a wrong way!) Let's see if we can find some patterns of asking that have been rewarded.

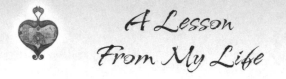

A Lesson From My Life

I've told you about the stormy days of my own marriage, when I was determined to keep all the mitzvahs despite the fact that my husband was not ready. When I had finally decided I was going to live my life as I chose, whether or not my husband was willing, the Rebbe warned me against it. The most important thing, he said, was to keep the mitzvah of Domestic Tranquility. It was more important that we grow together, in peace and mutual respect, than that I move ahead faster and alone.

I know now that my *demand* that my husband give me this independence was entirely wrong. The Rebbe's solution: I was to keep all the mitzvahs I was able to while maintaining peace in the home, and the rest would take care of itself. It was exactly right and taught me a powerful lesson. Please feel free to learn from my experience. *Forcing* your wishes on someone, making *demands* that benefit you but not necessarily anyone else, only hurts everyone else without benefiting you.

The "Fay" Way

Much like me at one time, Fay had become observant at a much quicker rate than her husband. And just as it had caused problems in my home, it was causing problems in her home.

"I'm so miserable!" she said. "I don't know what to do. I keep the Shabbat completely, and it's wonderful, but my husband insists on going to the office on Saturdays. It's so ridiculous; he owns the business and there is no point at all in his being there then. Yet no matter what I say or do, he insists he has to go in for a few hours on Saturday, and it really hurts. Our relationship is really suffering. I think he does this just because he knows it irritates me!"

I tried a couple of background questions. "What do you do on Shabbat mornings?" I asked. Fay eagerly responded, "I pray the Shabbat service. Then I study the weekly Torah portion. Then I read the entire book of Psalms, and sometimes I even study some of the Torah commentaries."

I saw the problem immediately. "It looks to me as if your husband is also suffering," I said. "He probably goes to the office because he's lonely and bored, and you are in your own world, wrapped in your prayers and studies. Nothing's wrong with prayer and Torah study, obviously, but remember:

Domestic Tranquility. Your husband has to come first." Funny how having heard those same words from the Rebbe, directed to me, helps when giving advice to someone else!

I went on to suggest an experiment: "Make a deal with your husband — men love deals! Tell him that you really miss him when he goes to work on Saturdays. Ask him to stay at home with you and you, in return, will spend the time with him and not even open a single book! Try this for four weeks and see what happens. People love pampering — find things to do and talk about that will nurture him, and you'll see. He will begin to look forward to Shabbat. As it is right now, he probably resents Judaism because he sees that it has taken you away from him. Remember, you were the one to first choose to be observant — now wait a little while for him to catch up!"

We talked some more, and I reinforced the idea that by using her feminine charm, making her husband feel wanted and loved and needed, she would soon be able to engage in all the Torah study and prayer she wanted — and he'd be right at her side.

It worked. But here's the real clincher: "I'd been praying for his soul," she cried. "I should have been praying for mine."

The wisdom of a lifetime, in thirteen words!

On Family

Little Ears And Big Mouths

On the evening of 3 Tammuz (the Rebbe's *yahrzeit*), I spoke in the main hall of Oholei Menachem (one of Crown Heights' large Torah schools for boys), sharing a few Rebbe stories of my own on modesty with a large crowd of women and girls.

One story began in 1979, when my husband and I moved from Milan, Italy, to Queens, New York. I was invited to stay in Crown Heights for Shabbat with a very dear, respected friend, an extremely pious woman. She and her husband both stem from respected religious families, and they are a wonderful couple.

After Friday night Shabbat dinner, I found myself sitting and chatting with her when she suddenly leaped up and rushed out of the room with her four-month-old baby boy, and immediately returned without him. Puzzled, I asked what was wrong. She explained that she does not allow her infant to hear anything even remotely negative. Even though we were not speaking forbidden speech, she nevertheless deemed our conversation inappropriate for the ears of her son and removed him promptly from the room. I never forgot it.

Over the years, we remained friends from afar, as she moved to another town. I continued to hold her in the highest esteem and we kept in touch occasionally by phone.

Just before 3 Tammuz of this past year, I enjoyed a pleasant surprise: a reunion. We sat next to each other at Oholei Menachem at a lovely wedding. As we reminisced and caught up with each others' lives, I mentioned that I had never forgotten that incident and that it continued to impress me with the importance of ethical speech education for our youth.

She looked at me for a few moments and then finally said: "If you remember it this many years, I really have to tell you the whole story. It was the Rebbe's instruction to me.

"When my baby was only three months old, my husband came home late one night. He is a rabbinical court judge and consequently has to deal with many different issues. Without dropping any names, he started to tell me about a religious divorce case he was involved in, while our baby was in the room.

"That night, I just could not sleep. It was bothering me. How could I possible have spoken about such a negative, wrenching topic in front of this pure, innocent little soul, my baby son? I had no peace. I resolved that I must write to the Rebbe, asking for a way to make spiritual amends. After much thought, I decided against telling my husband about my decision — I was sure he'd try to dissuade me from bothering the Rebbe with such a seemingly unimportant matter, and I really felt I had to ask the Rebbe.

"I duly wrote a letter the very next morning and gave it in at the Rebbe's office, feeling better already. I received a swift answer, one that shocked me. It came in two parts: '1. In the future, do not do this again. 2. Please publicize this matter to others.' "

"You followed the first part of the Rebbe's instruction so well," I interjected. "Maybe now it's time to keep the second part?" Maybe this is the reason we wound up sitting together at that wedding altogether! Who knows the ways of Divine Providence?"

So, with her permission, I have taken it upon myself to publicize this beautiful, important, meaningful teaching of the Rebbe, which will no doubt aid all of us in raising our children.

Too often we ignore our children when talking with other adults. We do not acknowledge that our children hear, absorb and are affected by our words, from birth onwards. It is wrong to assume that it is okay to say anything at all in front of babies, as they do not understand. Obviously, subconsciously, they *are* affected.

And the Rebbe wanted us to know this.

This illustrates how important modesty is — not only modesty of dress, but modesty in speech. Chassidic philosophy teaches that speech is one of the "garments of the soul," one of the methods by which the soul gains outward expression; like a person putting on clothing to go outside.

If the Rebbe emphatically teaches that it is not right for a baby of four months to overhear anything inappropriate, how much more so should we be careful in how we speak to our husbands, children, family, and friends, as well as, of course, the people we meet and introduce to Torah and mitzvahs.

It is taught, "[Giving] life and [causing] death are in the power of the tongue." May we use our awesome gift of speech to spread selfless love and cultivate unity.

Baba

There was once a couple who lived in Iran.

They were very good people, whose only wish was to raise good children who would walk in the path of Torah and mitzvahs. However, their wish remained unfulfilled. Each time they would have a child, the tender infant would pass away, may it never happen to anybody.

Finally, they were told by a kabbalist that when the next child would be born, they were to clothe him only in used clothes during his first year of life and adorn him with the pair of tiny gold hoop earrings he provided, and never to remove them. They followed these instructions scrupulously, and the next child – a beautiful baby boy – lived, to their great joy.

Years passed and the little boy grew up. He grew tired of people gawking at his earrings and of his friends laughing at the funny sight of a boy in jewelry. He demanded that the offending earrings be removed. His parents haplessly complied. To their terror, their son immediately grew sick and there seemed no hope of recovery. They were told by the kabbalist to put back the earrings to save their son's life. This time, they put one tiny earring in one ear, far above the lobe where it was less noticeable. Their son had an immediate and dramatic recovery and never removed that little earring for the rest of his life.

This story is true. The son was "Baba" (Farsi for "Daddy"), my father, Shmuel son of Pinchos, of blessed memory.

(When Baba came to visit me in New York, he was met with incredulous looks from some black people in Crown Heights — "Hey, this is some cool dude! Check out the earring!" We children were so accustomed to the earring that we tended not to notice it.)

Baba left Iran for Israel as a young man to find his fortune and a future wife. Soon he was introduced to mother, may she be healthy, and they were later married.

For economic reasons, they moved to Bombay, India, where there was a very large Jewish community of their fellow Iranian Jews, complete with *mikvah*, synagogue and all. They were very happy, and had four of their six children there, including me. The spiritual atmosphere was tolerant and good, and Torah was observed.

However, when India achieved independence from England in 1947, my parents emigrated — they did not want their children to be raised in the new milieu. After much discussion, they chose London. They would have preferred Israel, but opted for Great Britain instead, due to its stronger community and financial resources. I was two years old at the time.

Time went by and Baba was having serious financial troubles. He had depleted all his capital and could not find a decent job. He had been a very successful, well-respected rug merchant in India, supplying exquisite floorings to the likes of the Maharajah of Jaipur. But now Baba felt the pinch of hard times. With a big family and one more on the way (at the time, my mother was pregnant with my youngest sister Chana), my father was under pressure.

Baba wanted to be a jewelry broker, a job that did not involve investing money. If a merchant needed gems at £100 per carat, you would go to a supplier and get the goods for, say, £80 per carat. You would then sell them and receive a commission. It was a respectable job, and Baba saw people thriving in the business.

Unfortunately, no one would give him a chance, preferring instead to work with the more established brokers.

Baba would often go to the office of one Mr. Adler, the owner of a very successful jewelry firm, but to no avail. For six months, my father tried to get business from him. Finally, one fateful day, my father tried his luck with Mr. Adler again. As usual, he was told, "Thanks but no thanks." But this time, as he turned to leave, Mr. Adler told him, "Actually, I do need something that I see you have. Come back tomorrow and I'll give you a nice order."

Overjoyed, Baba left the office … and then suddenly stopped. It dawned on him that it was Friday — making "tomorrow" Shabbat (Mr. Adler was a completely secular Jew). Baba had been raised to be strictly Shabbat-observant and had never compromised Shabbat in any way. Now, G-d was giving him a difficult test.

"My wife is expecting a baby, I have no money left and I have so many mouths to feed!" Baba argued with G-d. "If I go in and tell this man that I will not go to him tomorrow, that's it! It'll be over!" But, of course, my Baba knew that he would not and could not ever go against the Torah. He simply would not work on Shabbat, G-d forbid.

Baba knocked quietly on Mr. Adler's door and crept in, apprehensive at the reaction he expected to receive. The man was sitting behind his desk, absorbed in his newspaper. He looked up.

"I'm sorry, but I will not be able to see you tomorrow."

Mr. Adler dropped the paper.

"It's been six months now that you've been nudging me for work. And now that I'm giving you a chance, you're refusing it! May I ask you *why?*"

Baba half expected to be thrown out of the office, but he said softly, "Because tomorrow is Shabbat and I never work on Shabbat."

At first, Mr. Adler had no reaction. He just sat there, rocking from side to side, thinking hard.

Finally, he broke the silence: "For six months you've been

asking me for work. Now that you get it, you won't do it because you don't work on Shabbat. For you, G-d comes before money. You don't sell your principles for money. From now on, I will do my business only through *you* — and anybody who wants to work with me will have to come through you. I now know that you are someone I can trust."

True to his word, Mr. Adler made Baba his right-hand man. He respected and trusted my father totally and, in turn, was never let down. My father's business ethics were exemplary. My late father-in-law always told people: "If I would give a million dollars to my *mechutan* (child's father-in-law) to take care of, I would sleep easily while he would anxiously watch over it!"

Years passed. And though Baba went through many trials and tribulations in his life, he always demonstrated an unbreakable love for Torah, G-d and his beautiful wife, my mother.

Every morning, usually at 5 a.m., he would rise and go to synagogue to put on tefillin – a mitzvah consisting of two small black boxes with black straps attached to them containing Biblical verses; Jewish men are required to place one box on their head and tie the other one on their arm each weekday morning – and pray. Afterward, he would study the Torah. Baba knew the whole Torah by heart and would often be the reader for the Torah in the synagogue.

I remember Baba always quoting from the Talmud. He would go to the men's *mikvah* every Friday afternoon before Shabbat. I was named Sarah because on the morning I was born, he was learning from that week's Torah portion about Sarah our Matriarch. He was quite a man; however, we children never truly appreciated his wisdom.

Once, when I told the Rebbe that Baba was ailing (by then, my parents were living in Israel), the answer was prompt and heartwarming: "In the *zechut* [merit] of your activities, your father will live a long life." Miraculously, my father recuperated and lived many more years.

Finally, at the age of eighty-seven, my beloved Baba returned his soul to his Maker, on 26 Tishrei, 5757 (Thursday, October 3, 1996), three days after the holiday of Simchat Torah. After a long life of integrity, Baba was laid to rest on the Mount of Olives, in an old Persian plot overlooking the slopes of Jerusalem. His six children all traveled to Israel for shivah – the seven-day mourning period in Jewish law for loss of immediate relatives – in my parents' home.

ℒ

Judaism teaches us that there is no "afterlife," as true life never ends — only the body ceases to have life. The soul lives on, watching over its loved ones.

A few years after Baba departed, my sister's son became a bar mitzvah, and my family went for the weekend to join the traditional bar mitzvah celebration in Worcester, Massachusetts, where my sister lived with her family. (They have since made aliyah - immigration to Israel - and now live in Jerusalem.) My husband and I were given one of our nephews' rooms.

That Friday night at her home, I felt cold and asked my sister for another blanket. Lying half asleep in bed in the very early Saturday morning darkness, I felt the blanket begin sliding off the bed. Just as quickly, I felt it somehow reposition itself back over me. I fell asleep comfortably once again, not thinking twice about the drifting blanket. I had been half asleep anyway.

Two weeks later, my husband told me that I must believe him, because he had witnessed the impossible. Out of character, he had a difficult time speaking, because he is very rational and not at all interested in the mystical, the occult or the supernatural. "I only believe what I can see," he says. He never makes things up and is extremely truthful.

Since the incident was so extraordinary and he felt no one would believe him, he waited two weeks before speaking of it.

On that Saturday morning in Worcester, he said, he was lying awake in his bed while I slept in the other bed a few feet away.

All of a sudden, the bedroom door opened. In walked Baba.

My husband was so shocked that he could not move or talk! He said that Baba picked up the blanket as it was slipping off my bed and laid it gently back over me. Then he turned to my husband and, smiling, put a finger across his own lips to signify that he should not make a sound.

At that point, my husband could not take it any more. He dived under his covers and lay there shivering with fright. When he finally came up for air, Baba was gone.

My husband is notorious for being very skeptical about exactly this kind of story, and he always states unequivocally that he does not believe them. Nevertheless, he vowed that he really saw Baba and that he definitely was not dreaming — although now he says he very well may have been. He says that my father appeared as he did in his younger, healthier days, and that he seemed very happy.

How do I explain it? Judaism teaches that the souls of our dear departed loved ones join their family's celebrations — and in rare exceptions, apparently, they engage in simple acts of love which are sometimes "caught on camera."

But of course our departed forebears are always watching over us — how can parents abandon their children?

On The Road

Great Strides In Great Britain

In mid-June 2003, I took a ten-day trip to Scotland. It felt so strange going back to Great Britain, where I grew up with no knowledge of Chabad. I set out with great excitement and eagerness.

I flew directly from New York to Glasgow to speak for a wonderful young Chabad couple, Rabbi and Mrs. Dovid and Sarah Cohen. A real one-woman powerhouse, Sarah infused me with an energy that blew away my jet lag in an instant.

Sarah found time to drive me down to the coastal fishing

town of Troon. What a majestic skyline! G-d's wonders were on full display. It was 11:30 p.m. and the sky was an extraordinary red color. To our right, it was dark. But to our left, it was still light, so ethereal and lovely. We were suspended between day and night.

The talk I gave the next day went well, thank G-d. After the talk, one man came up to thank me and put his hand out to shake hands. When I demurred, he could not believe it, and I explained the concept of Jewish modesty. I told him that male-female touch is only permitted between close relatives (parent-child, grandparent-grandchild, siblings), and between husband and wife only at certain times and in private. He was very intrigued, for it was (unfortunately) the first time that he had ever heard of such a thing. I also received a moving note from a Jewish nurse in attendance who became so overwhelmed with emotion that she could not speak to me afterward. I told her that I would read her note by the Ohel, the Rebbe's resting place.

I spoke at a different event during that same trip, at a different location, and there I noticed immediately that the Reform or Conservative rebbetzin in whose synagogue I would be speaking was very tense. As soon as I walked in, she asked me to make the talk very short. She did not seem happy. Then she sat down next to me on a sort of dais where I would speak.

Although my talk was mostly on Domestic Tranquility and Family Purity, questions were asked about the concepts of Divine Providence and Free Choice.

When I explained that the Baal Shem Tov taught that everything that happens is from G-d, the rebbetzin exploded right there on the stage. "I don't agree! Whatever happens is not from G-d, but from us!" she said, her face red with anger.

I immediately realized that she had obviously gone through a trauma of some sort, very recently.

The talk proceeded, but I felt so bad that I had somehow hurt the feelings of my fellow Jew. So, immediately after my talk, I approached her and apologized for saying something that had caused her pain. She burst into tears and hugged me. We stayed that way until she calmed down, and then she explained the reason behind her outburst.

"My son, who was twenty-nine years old, passed away two months ago," she choked out. "He was on strong medication for severe depression. One day he drank a whole bottle of alcohol and went for a drive. He died instantly in a car accident."

I was totally speechless. I could only hug her, wordlessly trying to comfort her.

She continued: "How could this have been G-d's doing?!"

After everyone had left, the rabbi's wife asked if she could please drive me to my hotel. Of course I agreed.

When we arrived, she got out of the car and told me: "I have been thinking about what you said. For months now, I have been tortured by the thought that my son's death was my fault. I could have helped him. I should have saved him. His death seemed like an unfortunate accident that could have been avoided! I had no rest. But if it is true that everything happens according to G-d's will, then I am not to blame. I finally feel that I should let go of this burden of guilt that I harbor and let my son rest in peace. I will accept this belief, because it takes a great weight off my shoulders."

I cried later that night, pondering my talk with this brave, unfortunate lady. I thought of my young daughter-in-law, of blessed memory, who was snatched away from us at such a tender age. Let Moshiach come and comfort us!

℘

At a third event, in London, a young woman with a baby approached me to discuss *mikvah* and whether or not to have more children. She was holistically inclined — she wanted to be a naturopath and heal people. I explained that the soul should be healthy first, and the body would follow suit. She should not neglect her soul's needs and should therefore keep the laws of Family Purity, I told her. She gladly took this mitzvah upon herself, though she had not even known about it previously. She asked about reading material and made arrangements to study under Mrs. Kinn or Mrs. Vogel.

Such is a Jewish soul: ready, willing and able to keep Torah and mitzvahs.

The entire trip was an eye-opening experience. Although I was not specifically asked to do so, I passed around a sheet for people to sign their names and mother's names each time I spoke. This list, I told them, will be given in to the Rebbe at the Ohel. The custom at the Ohel is to read letters or names of those needing blessings, tear the papers and place them on the grave site. Each place I went, the sheet was signed by everyone, and notes were also given to me to be read at the Ohel as well. My heart went out to all the people who wrote these notes, for their pain and suffering.

My trip also included a stop in Liverpool where I spoke for a group of couples organized by Rabbi and Mrs. Avrohom and Goldie Kievman. The Kievmans told me that some of the couples later asked to learn about the Jewish laws of Family Purity. The real excitement was yet to come. The house where Yisroel Aryeh Leib Schneerson, the Rebbe's late brother, once lived was pointed out to me. The Kievmans' son is named after the Rebbe's brother. Not since the Rebbe's brother lived there has there been another Yisroel Aryeh Leib in Liverpool.

Of all the places in England where I spoke, I felt very inspired in Manchester. There I spoke to a gathering organized by Lubavitcher women and others. It had been highly publicized in the newspapers. However, no one was prepared for the huge turnout! The hall was filled to capacity. There were at least 350 women there. What was symbolic of the future Messianic-era at this gathering was the blending of all types and forms of Jews: women in pants and Satmar Chassidic ladies with hats atop their wigs, Jewish converts and Sephardim (Middle Easterners),

Ashkenazim (of German heritage) and Italian, Irish and British women, all freely mingling and together for the sake of G-d and His mitzvahs. There was a wonderful feeling of unity. All these wonderful women had come out on a busy weeknight to listen to a woman whom they did not know talk about the Jewish concept of Domestic Tranquility! And some of them stayed to speak to me afterward for another hour.

As I stood up there on the stage and gazed out at the sea of wonderful faces, I felt a lump in my throat. I was so overcome with emotion. These are my sisters! We are all in exile together! We women will bring Moshiach now! How much longer, G-d?

"Heart" Times
On The West Coast

Although I am asked to speak, for the most part, at Lubavitcher establishments, sometimes I am invited to lecture for non-Lubavitch organizations. These invitations usually come from people who hear my talk and want me to speak for their people, like Mindy from Marin County.

This happened recently when I was speaking in San Francisco. The head of the community board in Seattle was present, and he asked me to speak for his community. After months of trying to coordinate schedules, I was finally able to fly out to do a *shabbaton* (Shabbat program) for them. I was put up in a magnificent home, with a full view of Lake Washington. It was very close to Bill Gates' home.

I would be speaking for an Orthodox, but definitely not Chabad, community. It was delicately hinted to me not to emphasize the Rebbe or Lubavitch too much, so as not to upset people. But the Rebbe found his way into my words, and the community's reaction was quite a revelation.

In my talks (I don't like the word "lecture"), I try very hard not to be preachy. I usually share stories about my personal experiences with the Rebbe. In this way, I feel that I convey the Rebbe's philosophy without making the audience feel I am imposing something on them. I simply share my own journey and hope they will join me. This time, too, I was loath to lose the opportunity for spreading the wellsprings of Chassidic thought. Why should anyone be deprived of the Lubavitcher Rebbe? And so I did what came naturally to me: I told stories of the Rebbe.

Although I was encouraged and heartened by the interest and emotion I saw on the faces of the audience, I was still not prepared for what was to come. In the question-and-answer period I usually give after my presentation, almost every question was about the Rebbe:

"Who was he?"

"What did he represent?"

"What are his teachings to us?"

"What made you close to him?"

"Tell us more about him!"

Chassidic philosophy – the "soul of the Torah" – truly sparks one's inner soul! It provides warmth and light in a world that has become spiritually darker and colder. Its teachings breathe new life and joy into the fulfillment of Torah and mitzvahs by tapping the inner resources of a Jew's soul. And by shedding light, it shows a Jew how to serve G-d beyond his normal capabilities, to transcend his limits.

Without it, members of other religious communities are left with a great hunger and thirst to know more about the true essence of G-d. The people sense that there is something out there, and when they are given a taste of Chassidism, they instantly recognize it as the truth and want more.

Nobody was upset with me for talking about the Rebbe and Chassidism. There's nothing like Chabad to ignite your soul and make you feel the true happiness of being a Jew. People pick up on this when you speak from your heart, and they react in kind.

Keeping Shabbat In Canada

I was once to speak for *shluchim* in Canada who asked if I would object to staying in the home of one of their community members. "The husband is very eager to keep Torah and mitzvahs," they told me, "but his wife is not cooperating. She is just not interested in Judaism. Please stay with them and try to influence her."

Now, in truth, I was going to speak at a *shabbaton,* and I was not so excited about staying in a home where I would not only be unable to eat, but would also have extra challenges with keeping Shabbat. But, of course, I accepted. Arrangements were made, and in due course I flew in and went to the home of my hosts. I was pleasantly surprised. Not only did the hostess receive me warmly, she also did not stop talking to me the entire Shabbat about Judaism in general and how to become more observant.

I could see how sincere she was, and I tried my best to simply be her friend and not just talk to her about what she should do. I felt strongly that she was ready to keep everything, but something was blocking her. I suspected that she was probably under too much pressure from her husband and was only resisting Judaism because it had to come from herself.

Finally, Shabbat was coming to an end. I was extremely tired from my trip, my speeches, talking to people and walking to and from the synagogue where I spoke.

I was praying the night service in a corner in my hostess' kitchen. I had decided that this was going to be the last time that I would stay with a non-Lubavitcher, simply because I feel that it is my duty to be well-rested and well-fed so that I can give it my all when I speak. It was very difficult to go for two days without enough rest or proper meals, and really the whole time "working."

Something happened that made me realize how wrong I was, and I felt ashamed of my decision.

Since I was praying *Shemoneh Esrei* (the silent petition), I could not move from my place. As such, I could not help but overhear a conversation that took place between my hostess and her young daughter. The little girl said loudly, "Mommy, the fridge light does not go on when I open the door!" Her mother mumbled something. Again, her daughter said, "Mommy, did you turn it off before Shabbat?" Her mother answered in the affirmative. "Mommy, did you do that because of our guest?" Her mother again said yes, softly. Triumphantly, the little girl said, "So Mommy, will we be doing this from now on? Will we be keeping Shabbat?"

I could hear Mommy's voice break as she told her daughter that yes, from now on they would be keeping Shabbat, and other mitzvahs, too. She was not the only one with a lump in her throat. After I finished praying, we had a wonderful talk, and I felt so happy that I had been privileged to meet this wonderful woman. She just needed to talk to someone, and I was honored to be the one to be there for her, to listen to her and encourage her. How rewarding to be able to see the success openly in front of me.

In many places I visit, I've realized that people open their hearts to me only because:

1. I am an older woman (experience counts);
2. I come from out-of-town so I am "safe" (i.e. they won't bump into me in the grocery store); and, most of all,
3. I have a blessing from the Rebbe.

And that – not my own effort – is what makes it all possible.

On Action

Shlichut: The World Of The Chabad Activist

From the outside, it may appear that all Chassidim are pretty much the same. Their dress is distinctive from mainstream Orthodox, but fairly similar among themselves. Most observe the mitzvahs with extra care, and all exhibit great reverence for their Rebbes.

However, there are some notable differences among the various groups. One of the ways in which Chabad Chassidim have become different from other groups of Chassidim in the last fifty years is in the Lubavitcher Rebbe's practice of "sending out," making emissaries of his Chassidim to reach out to other Jews.

For most Chassidim – Orthodox Jews who follow in the traditions of a particular Rebbe – one of their greatest joys is to be near their leader, the Rebbe. They consider it the greatest G-d-given privilege to be able to pray with him, study and learn with him, eat with him, or just engage in any common activity with him, so as to themselves become holier as they follow in the footsteps of their leader.

Chabad Chassidim share that desire too — there is little doubt that all of them, each and every one, would like to spend as much time as possible in the Rebbe's company. But the love a Chabad Chassid has for the Rebbe is expressed in a different way, especially nowadays. They recognize that the way to demonstrate your love for someone is to love the people that that someone loves. It's like a family. If you love your husband or wife, you love his or her parents … and brothers, sisters, aunts, uncles, and cousins — the whole family. Since your spouse loves them, so do you.

Similarly, say Chassidic teachings, since we love G-d, we also love whom G-d loves: all Jews, regardless of where they are or what they are doing. Thus, to demonstrate our love for G-d, we must love those He loves. If there is a far-off Jew – far away from Judaism, far away from his people, far away from G-d – what do you do if you love that Jew? You go to help! You help her with whatever she needs, including bringing her back to the family. You encourage her to rekindle a relationship with G-d, because ultimatcly, that is the only form of true happiness.

So for Chabad Chassidim, no matter how much they would

personally prefer to stay close to the Rebbe – to never be more than a walk away, to always enjoy the holidays and Shabbat in his presence – they agree to go away from him, some to the farthest, most remote corners of the Earth, perhaps for the rest of their lives. They will leave their Rebbe for one purpose only: to reach out to fellow Jews. This is the process of sending out *shluchim,* husband and wife emissaries, people who are sent out by the Rebbe to demonstrate G-d's love for every Jew with their very lives.

In modern times, this concept of sending representatives on *shlichut* (a mission) was conceptualized, designed and implemented by the Rebbe on a much larger scale then ever done by his predecessors. It was he who devised the plan for "lighting the lamps" of world Jewry — by sending out his own Chassidim, with their families, to establish Chabad centers all over the world.

Whom did he send? Several thousand young couples, some hardly out of their teens, many with growing families. Where were they sent? All over the world.

Many were sent to places where they didn't know anyone at all. Many were sent to places where they didn't even speak the local language. Today, any businessman who decided to expand his business internationally in that way would be regarded as insane. Yet, in Chabad-Lubavitch, the Rebbe's strategy was, and still is, wildly successful.

How did these young emissaries do it? With G-d's help, for

sure. The young couples willingly moved to their assigned part of the world and raised enough money to sustain themselves and their families. As soon as it was possible, they open a Chabad House, or outreach center, to serve the needs of every Jew in the area.

Today there are more than 4,000, (and growing!) Chabad-Lubavitch institutions in seventy countries all over the world — synagogues, schools, day care centers, outreach centers of every kind, from such remote and supposedly non-Jewish places as Hong Kong and Tunisia to the thousands scattered all over the United States, Europe, Central America, Australia and even Africa.

In 1994, there were, worldwide, several thousand Chabad institutions of all kinds. And since 1994 (the Rebbe's *yahrzeit*), over four hundred more *shluchim* have been sent to various parts of the world. The truth is, Chabad is growing more rapidly now than ever before in its history.

And the stories the *shluchim* tell! One can only imagine. Everyone on Earth has a story, and the *shluchim*, who seek out "lost" Jews in all parts of the world, tell some pretty miraculous tales.

One of the Chabad outposts I am most familiar with is the one in Bangkok, Thailand, because I accompany my husband on business there regularly. The Chabad House itself is hard to describe. You feel a spiritual power within its walls as soon as you walk through the door.

The contrast with the surrounding neighborhood is stark the streets all around are filled with lewd and immodest behavior. Just walking through, one sees and feels the myriad of much impurity. But the first sign you are getting close to Chabad is that you hear Chassidic music, and, like sounds from heaven, the music draws you in. The next hint is the aroma of cooking food — good, kosher food! There is a hint of home here, maybe a home you've never been to before, but one you remember all the same. As soon as you walk through the doors you sense the spirituality. I think you could be blindfolded three miles off, driven and led to the place without seeing a single thing, and still, once you stepped through those doors, you would know you were in a place where G-d feels at home.

If I were to create the image of perfect emissaries, it would be much like Rabbi Nechemia Wilhelm and his "woman of valor," Mrs. Nechomie Wilhelm. Just like our Patriarch Abraham, and Sarah his wife, these young people welcome all who pass their way, inviting them into their realm of peace and holiness. The Chabad House in Bangkok is famous among Israelis — many of whom are not at all observant, but who come regularly to Chabad, just for a taste of home. Once there, they are welcomed with open arms, fed and treated to the best *shluchim* of all, the Wilhelms' children: Menachem, who is ten years old; Chani, eight; Devorah, six; Chaim, four; Sari, two; and Rivkah, who is six months old. The children are irresistible, and never fail to charm even the shyest visitor.

At the most recent Passover, there were over two hundred people at the Seder — almost all of them Israelis, and for many of them, it was their first Seder! I sometimes think that G-d must take particular delight in the irony of Jewish Israelis, traveling in Bangkok, finally join in their first Jewish celebration of our freedom!

One would understandably think that from 1994 onwards, when the Rebbe's physical presence was removed from us, Lubavitcher Chassidim the world over would return to Crown Heights. Every Lubavitcher would prefer to live in the neighborhood where the Rebbe had once lived, so their children could attend Crown Heights' "big city" Jewish schools and stroll its very Jewish streets.

But this, exactly, is what worldwide Chabad is all about. Chabad Chassidim's love for their Rebbe keeps them at their posts, which is surely where he would want them.

Shmuel's Freedom

I was eating at the Chabad House Restaurant in Bangkok. (Real Israeli food!) My waiter was a friendly young *sabra* (slang for native-born Israeli) named Shmuel. He had pierced eyebrows, earrings and a long bushy ponytail that looked a little odd with his yarmulke, but his smile was one thousand watts of pure sincerity. It wasn't long before I heard his story:

Some time previously, Rabbi Wilhelm had been walking in downtown Bangkok and had run into Shmuel. Discovering that he was Jewish, the rabbi invited him to put on tefillin and say the *Shema Yisrael* prayer on the spot. Shmuel's reaction was both swift and sharp. He snapped at Rabbi Wilhelm to leave him alone, saying that he thought all religion was hypocrisy and that no matter what happened, he never wanted to see him again. Rabbi Wilhelm went on his way.

A few weeks later, word got to Rabbi Wilhelm that the Thai police had arrested a young Israeli Jew on suspicion of drug trafficking — something that might be a death-penalty offense if proven. Rabbi Wilhelm did what a *shliach* must do. He located the filthy, uninhabitable hole in the ground prison where the Israeli was being kept, and was astonished to discover the young man who had screamed at him some weeks before to get lost.

At this point, Shmuel's attitude changed — he was powerfully embarrassed at the way he had treated the rabbi before, and now, he assumed, the rabbi would let him sit there in that prison, just to show him the error of his ways.

But the Chabad *shliach* did exactly the opposite, of course. Right away, Rabbi Wilhelm promised that he would get Shmuel released somehow, and that he would not rest until did. And there were no conditions: Shmuel was free to do as he chose after that. Still, Shmuel didn't believe it. He was sure he would owe the rabbi some huge debt, until he was actually released several days later. The rabbi had pulled out all the stops, found the right influential people, and paid the right bribes.

When Shmuel was released, he was so embarrassed that he wept, begging Rabbi Wilhelm to forgive him, even as he struggled to believe what had just happened: a rabbi, upon whom he had poured vitriol and insult in public, had just spent several days and a considerable amount of his own money to have a nonobservant and decidedly antireligious Jew he didn't know at all released from prison.

Once freed, Shmuel wanted to know more about this kind of goodness. He asked if he could study with Rabbi Wilhelm and if there was anything he could do to help out at Chabad House. Yes on both counts was the answer.

About a year and a half later, Shmuel returned to Israel and is now part of an observant community — all because he got to experience, firsthand, the kind of unconditional love that G-d (and those who love Him) can show to a fellow Jew.

"Right Now!"

Rabbi Wilhelm has a very long arm. It stretches all the way to Israel.

The rabbi's brother-in-law, Moshe Alter, lives in Israel. Moshe Alter had purchased a refrigerator and was waiting for it to be delivered. The young deliveryman wheeled the fridge into Moshe's lobby and was climbing the stairs to figure out how best to haul it up, when he suddenly stopped, looked at his watch and ran back to the van. A minute later, he reappeared with a pair of tefillin, and asked if it would be okay if he took a break to put on the tefillin and pray.

Moshe Alter was surprised. Apparently the deliveryman didn't look very much like someone who would put on tefillin at all, let alone to be so scrupulous about it. When he inquired, the deliveryman told him that he was strict about putting on tefillin ever since he had been to Bangkok and talked with a Rabbi Wilhelm there at the Chabad House. "Rabbi Wilhelm," he said, "told me how important it is for me to put on tefillin every day, on time, and so now I never miss it!"

The deliveryman was excited to learn that Moshe Alter was Rabbi Wilhelm's brother!

No More "Anti"

Barak also had an encounter with the legendary Rabbi Wilhelm. Barak, another young Israeli who went to Bangkok to "find himself," wandered the Far East until he stumbled upon Rabbi Wilhelm at the Chabad House. He would hang around from early morning to late at night, asking questions, questions and more questions.

The questions were all of the "What is the meaning of life?" persuasion — the kind of thing many of us pass through at some point in our lives. Barak wanted to know what true riches were, what satisfaction was, what the purpose of life was and how he could find happiness. He had finally decided that Buddhism was the way to go — after all, if you just removed yourself from the world, then you couldn't be unhappy about your place in it, presumably. If you had no wife, home, job or responsibilities, then you wouldn't have to worry about losing any of them.

Rabbi Wilhelm managed a one-man re-education campaign on young Barak, explaining that removing yourself from the world was exactly the opposite of what G-d wanted. What G-d wanted – and the one thing that would make a Jew like Barak happy – was for him to involve himself in the world, using his own strengths and resources to transform it and make it a place for G-d to dwell in. Leaving the world with all its problems behind would never result in happiness; only frustration, longing and ultimately bitterness for all the things he would eventually be lacking.

Barak listened, and then decided he would go to Burma to make up his mind. He would be, he said, one of two things: either a Buddhist or adherent to Chabad. Like Moshe (see *"The Coincidence of a Name,"* above), who had put before him the choice of life or death, Barak had clear options.

Barak's story is not over. All this is recent and he is still deciding.

In the wake of Barak, another young Israeli appeared at Rabbi Wilhelm's door, this one named Kfir. Unlike Barak, who was still searching, Kfir had already made up his mind. He was, Rabbi Wilhelm said, one of the most Jew-hating Jews he had ever met. He was against everything and anything that had anything to do with Judaism, and had no inhibitions whatsoever about saying so to Rabbi Wilhelm — who spent several hours listening and talking, all to no avail.

Or so it seemed. Kfir went away, seemingly as bitter and angry as he had arrived — better educated, perhaps, but no less hostile. Then one day, a fax arrived in Bangkok. Rabbi Wilhelm let me read it. What follows is a translation from the Hebrew:

Dear Rabbi Wilhelm,

When I left Bangkok, I really wanted to tell you about all those long talks we had. I want you to know I am not dati (religious) or a believer in anything, and I'm still pretty much ignorant of Judaism. But I have something to tell you.

I was, just like you said, "anti-everything." I was anti-religion, anti-yarmulke, and anti just about anything you brought up. But you didn't try to brainwash me, and you didn't threaten me. You were just my friend. I am writing to tell you that even though we have different ideologies and backgrounds, I really respect and admire you.

Rabbi, you took away all my "anti"!

Your friend,
Kfir

So what do you see here? I see a soul who has made great progress. Who knows what G-d has in store for either Barak or Kfir? Our prayer is that they each move from strength to strength, and finally find the path that leads all the way home.

The Path Of Ronen

Kfir and Barak are still out there somewhere, but Ronen found the way.

Ronen was another young Israeli, but not quite so lost, perhaps, as the other two. Ronen wasn't wandering, trying to find himself. He was a businessman who had stopped in Bangkok on his way to Japan, where he was just about to open a branch of his business.

On that Bangkok stopover, Ronen took a breather at the Chabad House — kind of a strange thing to do, because Ronen was completely nonobservant and had no family experience of Jewish tradition of any kind. But during that first trip, he met with two of the young rabbinical students who were in Bangkok at the time, Itzik and Schneur, and they got to talking. Soon, on every trip through, Ronen took a stopover at Chabad, and little by little he began keeping mitzvahs. First he put on tefillin, then he began a hesitant observance of keeping kosher, and so on, and every day, the importance of these ideas grew in Ronen's mind and merged into his life.

Ronen was doing very well indeed in his business. He was now buying silver jewelry in Thailand, where he could buy very cheaply, and selling it in Japan. There was that one moment in time when everything seemed ready to converge: the exchange rate, the purchase prices, the waiting customers in Japan. Everything was perfect. He was about to make a fortune.

But, all at once, everything seemed to go wrong. The first disaster was when the immigration authorities sent all his workers back home and he couldn't find anyone local to do the job. Then he was evicted from his place of work on some trumped-up excuse. His business partner told him he was ready to quit — he couldn't handle all these problems any longer.

And the last straw? Ronen's girlfriend told him she was in love with someone else. At that point Ronen started to envy Job and his famous struggles — at least he had a loyal wife!

Ronen went to Rabbi Wilhelm, depressed, distraught and disappointed. "How could all this be happening?" he wanted to know. After all, he was becoming more and more observant — why were all these disasters happening now, when he was trying to do everything right?

They talked for many hours, but in the end, the solution seemed clear to Rabbi Wilhelm. "You must close your business on Shabbat," he told Ronen. "If you do that, your business will improve."

Now this, to a man whose business is floundering anyway, does not sound like a good idea. "How can I close my business, Shabbat or not?" Ronen wanted to know. "My income is already way down — how can I give up a dollar more of business?"

Rabbi Wilhelm assured him that if he closed his business on Shabbat, his income would improve. He begged Ronen to just try it and see. "How about no Shabbat business for one month?" he suggested. "A whole month?" groaned Ronen. It felt like too much, but in the end Ronen agreed: He would close for one month, but only if his partner agreed. If he would say no, then there would be no deal.

Rabbi Wilhelm wasted no time. Off he went to the business partner. He explained the situation and his personal guarantee to Ronen, and asked for a one-month test. The partner, maybe thinking that by this point there was not much to lose, agreed. One month.

Three weeks later the fax machine starting warbling, and out slid a note from Ronen:

Dear Rabbi Wilhelm,

As you asked, I am writing to let you know how everything is going. We have been closed on Shabbat for three weeks now, and everything is more than okay. Not only have our troubles stopped, but money is coming in — more than we could ever have expected. The blessings you promised are materializing.

Thank you for guiding me!
Ronen

Rabbi Wilhelm still gets calls from Ronen, telling him more good news every time. Now fully observant, Ronen's life has taken on not only material blessings, but a whole new purpose and vitality.

What a G-d we have! He constantly rewards every little attempt of ours. If only we would just trust Him more.

The Mitzvah Of
The NonKosher Soup

This story took place several years ago, before Rabbi Wilhelm had been sent to Bangkok. But it's a story that could be reported from almost anywhere, even today.

Akiva was a very successful businessman in Bangkok. He and his family had been relatively traditional when they arrived in the Far East, but for a number of reasons – the difficulty of getting kosher food, the few Jews around for company and strength – their observance began to slip, and then disappeared altogether. Some remnants of Judaism may have remained, like the mezuzah on their door, but one thing that disappeared altogether was keeping kosher.

Akiva was eating anything and everything. In particular, there was a kind of Thai soup he absolutely loved — I will refrain from telling you exactly what was in it, but you can guess. And it goes without saying that it was decidedly nonkosher.

One day, Akiva had to go on a business trip to Hong Kong, and somehow, while there, he met up with Rabbi Mordechai Avtzon, the Rebbe's *shliach* to that city-state. They began talking, and Rabbi Avtzon asked how things were in Bangkok. Was Akiva able to get kosher food? What other supplies were available? Akiva told Rabbi Avtzon very honestly that he no longer kept kosher, but also told him how impossible it was to find kosher food. There was simply no kosher meat or poultry, he said.

Rabbi Avtzon heard the last part – how difficult it was to get food – but either didn't hear, or chose to ignore, the part about Akiva's not keeping kosher. Instead, he told Akiva that he would see what he could do about having some kosher food, at least meat and chicken, sent to him.

Akiva was very impressed. He thought it was very nice that some stranger would care so much about him. As he listened to more of the difficulties Rabbi Avtzon was facing – a lack of heat in the home to hold off the cold winter being only part of the problem – he became more and more impressed. "Why would this man who obviously has problems of his own care so much about me?" he wondered.

The two soon parted, and Akiva went home. He remembered the rabbi's promise about finding kosher meat for him, but he decided it must be like one of those things you say to new acquaintances, you know, like, "Let's have lunch," even though no one has any real intent to get together for lunch, ever. And then, too, old habits are hard to break. That Thai soup was beckoning, and he ate — not only the soup, but other non-kosher food as well.

Some time later, Akiva was in his office, right about

lunchtime (just about to sit down to a bowl of his favorite soup, actually), when his telephone rang. Who was it? None other than Rabbi Avtzon calling from Hong Kong. "Good news!" the rabbi said. "I've found a way to have frozen kosher meat shipped to you, and I wanted to tell you when to expect the shipment!"

Akiva hung up, stunned. How was it possible? How could this man, with a whole family to care for, with a new religious center he was trying to run, with no heat in his own home, go out of his way to find, order, pay for and ship kosher meat to a man he had met only once? It was unbelievable, just unbelievable.

Akiva looked down at his bowl of half-eaten nonkosher soup, the soup he loved so much and couldn't get enough of. Suddenly the soup didn't look very good anymore. In fact, it looked pretty disgusting. "And why would I eat that soup anyway?" he wondered. His new friend in Hong Kong was shipping him *real* food — good food, fit for a Jew! He could not wait.

Akiva picked up the bowl of soup, spoon and all, took it to the trash can and dumped it in, never to be seen again. And then he went to the bathroom and rinsed out his mouth.

When that was done, he promised himself, "Never again. From now on, I will eat only kosher food. When G-d decides He cares enough about what I eat to send a rabbi all the way from Hong Kong to arrange kosher food for me, the least I can do is eat it." And he did. Akiva and his family returned to keeping kosher right then, and within a short while, to full observance.

See what a dedicated lamplighter can do in those remote parts of the world? The souls of these "lost" Jews *want* to be lighted — but someone has to go out there and do it.

The $1,800 Lulav And Etrog

The *shluchim* of Bangkok maintain very close ties with the *shluchim* in Hong Kong. On the eve of the holiday of Sukkot, especially close contact was kept in order to obtain and be able to fulfill the mitzvah of assembling together the *lulav* (palm frond), *etrog* (citron), *hadassim* (myrtle twigs) and *aravot* (willow twigs).

Usually, before Sukkot, the regional Israeli Embassy would arrange for a *lulav* and *etrog* for the Jews living in Thailand. However, one year, nothing was provided. Finally, three days before Sukkot, Rabbi Kantor (the head *shliach* in Thailand) and Mr. Avraham Kashani (a community pillar) called Rabbi Avtzon in Hong Kong to ask for a *lulav* and *etrog*, only to be told that one was available, but without the willow twig. By the morning of the day before Sukkot they had the *lulav, etrog,* and *hadassim,* but … still no *aravot.* All four were necessary in order to fulfill the mitzvah.

Finally, some turned up in Hong Kong. "Send them over immediately with anyone who has a valid visa," pleaded Rabbi Kantor, "and we'll pay for their flight!" Rabbi Avtzon started frantically calling everyone. Anyone. They all thought that he had completely gone crazy, willing to pay $1,800 between air-fare and courier's fees just to bring over some "vegetables"!

But at the last minute, someone agreed to do it. However, he was involved in an accident on the way to the airport and missed his flight. The next flight out was at 3 p.m. and was full. Sukkot was at 6 p.m.! But, thank G-d, at last he found one seat, and took the two-hour flight to Thailand.

Now, Bangkok is notorious for its horrendous traffic jams, and one can sometimes be stuck for four hours during rush hour. To avoid getting stuck, as rush hour coincided with the time the courier would land, a motorcyclist was sent to pick him up.

Just when everyone thought the crisis was over, disaster struck again. The King of Thailand chose to go out at that time, and, of course, all the roads were immediately closed to everyone, including our motorcyclist! Frantic phone calls went back and forth, and the man who was given $1,800 to bring the strange "vegetable" had the wits to take the train.

Finally, Rabbi Kantor had the *lulav, etrog, haddasim* and box of *aravot* in his possession, and with trembling hands, he opened the box. To his dismay, instead of fresh, soft green leaves, the leaves were dry, curled up and crumbly. He had to do a lot of fast reading in the *Shulchan Aruch* (Code of Jewish Law) before he could pronounce them kosher. But, thank G-d, they were acceptable even in that state, and he finally had the *arbaah minim* (Four Species) with which to fulfill a mitzvah of Sukkot.

Rabbi Kantor said that this was a big lesson to him. Although he always knew that each and every Jew is necessary, and equal, this openly shows that just as the *etrog, lulav and had-*

dasim are not complete without the *aravot*, even if they are dry and appear worthless, so too we the Jewish People cannot be complete without even the simplest, "dry" Jew, whom indeed the willow represents.

We, too, have to search for him, and even go to expense and trouble for him.

Sheldon

All prayers are answered; not all are answered in the way we expect. Such is the lesson of Sheldon.

Some time ago, people in 770 were mystified to hear the Rebbe reciting Kaddish — the beautiful prayer of praise for G-d recited to bolster the soul of the deceased. No one knew for whom it was intended, as no one from the Rebbe's family had passed away on this date, as far as anyone knew.

In 1981, a friend of mine asked me to help Baruch Nachshon, the famous Chassidic artist of Kiryat Arba, Israel. Mr. Nachshon was in the U.S. to promote his lovely artwork — spectacular paintings that do so much to visually impart deeper spiritual meaning into parts of the Torah. I had called another friend, who had another acquaintance, who suggested that the thing to do to help Mr. Nachshon was to go see Sheldon, a powerful Jewish business leader in his sixties. The necessary connections were made, and one day shortly thereafter we all made the trip to Long Island to Sheldon's exquisite, lavish mansion. It was quite a place — set on acres of land, dotted with racehorse stables and tracks, a swimming pool, helicopter pad, every element of luxury one could imagine.

As we drove up, Sheldon and his non-Jewish wife came out

to meet us. He was visibly surprised to see Mr. Nachshon, who was obviously observant — tzitzit (ritual fringes) dangling from beneath his shirt, together with a long beard and yarmulke, will give a man away every time. Nonetheless, Sheldon quickly overcame his initial shock and grandly showed us around his estate. The tour was fascinating, but we were dismayed – beyond dismayed – to see his private chapel filled with stained glass depicting very non-Jewish themes, plus a lot of statues everywhere that could only be called idols. Sheldon could see that we were uncomfortable, but I don't think he could understand why we would be so distressed at seeing how far away this brother of ours had fallen.

Nonetheless, we had our mission. When, after a time, we had to leave, our preliminary business arrangements were wrapped up and a second visit was arranged. Mr. Nachshon asked if at that time he could bring mezuzahs for the doors, and Sheldon quickly agreed, somewhat to our surprise. When we arrived the next time, we affixed the mezuzahs to the doors with the proper blessings, and Sheldon seemed to be delighted. In fact, when Mr. Nachshon suggested that they put on tefillin and say the Shema, Sheldon again was happy to oblige. We had brought along some kosher treats for us all, and I could see that Sheldon was genuinely happy to have been reintroduced to his heritage. It was as though a starving soul had been given a taste of life-restoring food, and was responding with all the strength it had. We took photos of a proud Sheldon.

We did notice, however, that Sheldon's wife had become far less bubbly. She had begun to see what *could* happen if something weren't done to stop it, and soon.

When we left this time, we asked Sheldon if he would like to come to the Rebbe for Dollars one Sunday. He enthusiastically said yes.

A couple of weeks later we picked up Sheldon, and his uncle who wished to join us, and drove to 770. At the meeting with the Rebbe, Sheldon was overwhelmed, tears streaming down his face. The Rebbe thanked him most graciously for helping Mr. Nachshon, and then turned to Sheldon's uncle, handed him a dollar, and gave him a blessing for restoration to health. "How did he know I am about to have an operation?" he asked. Both Sheldon and his uncle were astounded.

I genuinely liked Sheldon, and we kept in touch. One time we took Sheldon to Mermelstein's restaurant in Crown Heights for lunch. Afterward, we walked down Kingston Avenue, through the heart of Chabad in Crown Heights. Sheldon had such a good time, reminiscing about his childhood and his family, which had been traditional. Not too long after I invited him for Shabbat. He seemed to enjoy every minute, from the lighting of the candles on Friday evening to the steaming *cholent* on Shabbat. Sheldon fit right into our family, and I could see he felt that way, too. Our home was a warm Jewish home, not at all like the fancy showplace he shared with his non-Jewish wife and the cold statues made of plaster and paint.

And we talked, of course. We never stopped talking. Sheldon's first wife had been Jewish, and they had a son who married a Jewish woman and had a child. To Sheldon's great sorrow, his son became involved with another woman and divorced his first wife. He eventually married the other woman – a non-Jew – and converted to her religion. Sheldon was heartbroken. With difficulty, I refrained from making any observation about how the son had only followed in his father's footsteps. There was, however, one big difference — Sheldon had never denied his Jewishness, and was hugely supportive of Israel although he'd never been there. One day, he said, he would go visit. It was the true home of every Jew, he said.

Several months later Mr. Nachshon returned from Israel with several of the paintings Sheldon had commissioned. By this time, Sheldon was in a state of torment as everything that his wife had feared was coming true. Sheldon's reintroduction to his own traditions was taking hold – what he wanted now, for what likely were his last years, was to live an observant lifestyle with its riches and beauty.

As a result, his home life had quickly become miserable — he confided that he now knew his wife had married him only for his money, and to some extent he was afraid of her. She would never let him go, because she considered his massive wealth her inheritance, and she would have it, one way or another.

Poor Sheldon. He would call once in a while, for no apparent purpose. But I know what he wanted: he just wanted to be reassured that he was, when all was said and done, still a Jew. He had not lost the essence of his being, of who he was, when all else was stripped away.

What a pitiable situation, steeped in irony. Here was this hugely wealthy Jewish man, a man who could afford what most of us cannot, living in a prison of sorts, guarded over by his non-Jewish wife who was dedicated to the idea that he have no connection to his Jewish soul. The one thing he desperately wanted, he could not get for love or money.

Although he was constantly guarded by security men, locked gates, cameras and three large dogs, he never felt safe, because he was not truly loved and valued. He was not happy. The curse of too much wealth served a very sad purpose.

One day I heard the shocking news: Sheldon had passed away the night before. I rushed to his home on Long Island, appalled to see that the wife had dressed Sheldon's body in his best suit, and had him laid out in an open casket in that hideous "chapel," surrounded by the hideous stained glass and idols. I wept for Sheldon, for his poor tortured soul, and for all that he, and we, had lost. The wife outlined her plans: Sheldon would lie in state for four days, until Monday, when they would hold the funeral. A lost soul!

Chabad to the rescue! I called Rabbi Anchelle Perl, the nearest Chabad *shliach*, and never have you seen such efficiency. The one important thing Sheldon had done before his death was to arrange to be properly buried in a Jewish cemetery. That was all Rabbi Perl needed. Together with a friend of Mr. Nachshon, he swiftly and with great firmness put together a whole, legally correct Jewish funeral – despite the VIP police escort – to beat the other one the wife had in mind. The Jewish funeral would take place that very day, as required by Jewish law. Two very special people present at the funeral were Sheldon's Jewish (former) daughter-in-law and his Jewish granddaughter. Sobbing, the young girl asked me if she could say Kaddish for him. This ex-family of Sheldon's was, so far as I could tell, the only family who had ever really loved him.

It was at exactly this time that the Rebbe was heard saying Kaddish for someone. Was it for Sheldon?

May the soul of poor Sheldon find peace and rest. His life has many lessons for all of us — about priorities, about the importance of heritage, about how little time we may have to make things right. It is never too early, or too late, to begin the trek back home to your own people.

Out Of Iran

When I went to see my dear mother in Israel recently, her friend came over to visit, and told me a story. With her permission, I now tell it to you.

In a town in Iran, there once lived a pious Jewish woman. On a pilgrimage to Israel, she prayed by the grave of King David. She vowed that if G-d would grant her a baby and it would be a son, she would name him David, after the great king. To her great happiness, she soon found that she was expecting a child. Her joy was short-lived, however, as she soon became severely ill with typhus. The doctors informed her that the medications she needed, as well as the sickness itself, were certain to produce a child that would probably not survive. If the baby did survive, she was told, it was likely to be abnormal.

Several weeks passed and the doctors informed her that they could not detect a heartbeat. The baby was not alive, and she would need to have the fetus removed. With a heavy heart, she made the appointment to go in the next day for the procedure.

That night, her anguish made sleep difficult. How could she do such a thing? What if the baby were still alive? But the doctors said it was over, and had given her no hope! Finally, still tormented by doubts, she fell into a deep, exhausted slumber.

In her sleep, she dreamed she was holding a beautiful, happy baby boy in her arms. As she was smiling down at her son, a group of rabbis with glowing faces, led by one particular rabbi, approached her and gently took her son from her arms with the words, "Your son belongs to us." A moment later, they walked away with the baby.

She awoke in a state of excitement and confusion. The dream had seemed so real, the people so real, the baby so real! Had it all been just a dream?

She went to her appointment, and the doctors duly examined her before doing the surgery — and to their great amazement, they heard the unmistakable sound of a loud, strong heartbeat. They immediately cancelled the surgery but continued to warn her that it was highly doubtful that the child would be healthy. But the dream of the rabbis with the luminous faces reassured the woman that she would have a healthy baby, and she refused to believe the doctors. Unafraid, she was filled with hope and joy.

In due time, the woman gave birth to a healthy baby boy, and her joy knew no bounds. She and her husband raised their son, Dovid, named as promised after King David, to be a good, kind child with excellent character traits. His community and family loved him dearly.

With the 1979 rise of Khomeini and his Islamic Revolution, the Rebbe sent his people to save Jewish children, and the woman was approached and advised to send her son to

America. She asked these Jewish strangers why they cared about Iranian children, and why they had come all the way from America to save them. In response, she was shown a picture of the Rebbe — and she almost fainted on the spot. This was the leader of the holy men she had seen in her dream of years ago, a dream she had never forgotten.

Having been introduced to the Lubavitcher Rebbe, she now refused to send her precious son away. The first part of the dream had come true. She now feared the second: "I know that if I send him away, I will never, ever, get him back." But the situation in Iran so deteriorated that she realized she had no choice — because she loved her son, she sent him out of her life to freedom, hoping that he would be raised lovingly by these others and praying to be reunited with him one day.

Young Dovid came to Brooklyn, studied for years in Jewish seminary and became an earnest scholar, and, in the summer of 1990, married Ronit, a fine young Jewish woman of Moroccan heritage.

Shortly after they married and settled in Crown Heights, Ronit conceived but had a problematic pregnancy. She was prescribed seven months of bed rest to prevent miscarriage.

Understandably, the young couple went to the Rebbe for Dollars.

When their turn in line came, Dovid told the Rebbe that his wife needed a blessing. *"Brachah v'hatzlachah* – blessing and success," smiled the Rebbe. He handed Dovid a dollar. Then the Rebbe gave Ronit a dollar. They turned to leave.

Moments later, Rabbi Groner (the Rebbe's aide) called out, "The Rebbe has not finished with you yet!" Ronit hurried back to hear the Rebbe say *"refuah shleimah! –* A complete recovery!" The Rebbe then handed her two more dollars.

The pregnancy was uneventful from that moment on; the problems simply disappeared. Baby boy Yosef Yitzchok was delivered healthily seven months later, followed over the next several years by little girl Chaya Mushka and her younger brother Menachem Mendel. Considering Ronit's chronic heart problems, her doctors were amazed that she carried even one child to full term in good health, let alone three. But the Rebbe's three dollars had turned into three beautiful blessings.

And to compound the blessing, Dovid's parents finally escaped Iran and moved to Israel. The only problem now was the young couple's lack of livelihood and great financial hardship.

Years later, Dovid's father tragically perished in a car accident in Israel. His mother traveled to New York to spend some time with her son and his family, and perhaps find some consolation. But soon after arriving and seeing the dire financial situation, she made a determined trip to the Ohel.

Standing at the Rebbe's resting place with all the pure faith and trust and love she had for him, she reminded him simply: "You told me that my son belongs to you! So it is your job, then, to help him with sustenance. Please, Rebbe, help him support his wife and children!"

The very next day, Rabbi Dovid Loloyan was hired by the Chabad Persian Center in the Valley (of Southern California), a position he holds to this day. Now a highly respected, deeply beloved rabbi, teacher and head of a community, Rabbi Loloyan truly belongs to the Lubavitcher Rebbe, helping his flock and his students around the clock in any way possible, living his life in answer to a long-ago dream in far-away Iran.

Changing The Jewish World

This travelogue was originally published in the December 1999 issue of the N'shei Chabad Newsletter.

I am once again in Thailand with my husband, and I am inspired by the magnificent work that Chabad is doing here. The Rebbe's work is being carried out in full force by the local *shluchim*, who truly live his message.

Rabbi Yosef Chaim Kantor and his admirable wife, Nechamah, go above and beyond the call of duty. Among his other accomplishments, Rabbi Kantor slaughters kosher chickens for the whole community in the sweltering heat of Bangkok. They even have a kosher bakery now. On Shabbat day, he walks for over one hour from his home to the synagogue on the other side of Bangkok — in his traditional black coat and hat, in the humidity and fiery heat! At the synagogue, he introduces young Jews to the wisdom of Judaism through his erudite Torah talks. They also have a preschool and have renovated the old community *mikvah*. Great job!

The Israeli Chabad House run by Rabbi Wilhelm and his tireless wife, Nechomie, is also a unique institution, located in one of the most impoverished neighborhoods of Bangkok. This Chabad House has become a home away from home for hundreds of Israeli lost souls who go to Thailand to find themselves. They find spirituality in this most unique Chabad House, nestled among dilapidated guest houses. One need only look at the shining, holy faces of these wonderful young *shluchim* to appreciate their true dedication and love for their fellow Jews.

Seeing all these young Israelis sitting, talking, eating like one big family is an unforgettable experience. Sometimes one does a double-take realizing that these are Jews, as their dress, hairstyles, tattoos, body piercing and the like are truly very far from what a holy nation should look like. These accessories have become so fashionable that they are considered the norm instead of rebellious. Some of the girls have such innocent faces that one wants to just reach out and clean off the superfluous *shmutz* (grime) to reveal the hidden Jewish soul.

Chasidism teaches that no Jew can ever deny his or her Jewishness. Even the lowest of the low cannot commit idol worship. How true, and how vividly this lesson was brought home to me! I witnessed time and again how these youngsters would walk into the Chabad House as if they were walking into an oasis. They greeted Rabbi Wilhelm as if he was part of their family, with broad, beaming smiles and even hugs.

I could not help noticing one young Israeli man whose whole appearance was particularly garish. He sported wild, curly hair hanging down his back, tied up in the ubiquitous ponytail that seems to be the Israeli uniform abroad.

His whole air was very bohemian, to put it mildly.

However, what a lesson I learned, and how ashamed of my first impression, when this young man left the Chabad House! As he stepped out, he turned and looked carefully for the mezuzah on the door. He kissed it with such tenderness and love that it brought a lump to my throat.

How good are your people, G-d! Please bring Moshiach and redemption already! We're all polished and ready, even though we are sometimes "diamonds in the rough."

I noticed so many young men automatically reach out for one of the yarmulkes kept by the door and un-self-consciously put them on, sometimes insisting that their friends put them on as well. How incongruous they looked with their flimsy Thai-style clothing and earrings. But wear them they did, and with great pride. No one can deny their inherent Jewishness.

Rabbi Wilhelm is drawing close these young Israelis for one important reason: pure, unconditional love of a Jew! His goal is not to chalk up one more person who puts on tefillin, but just to change the negative perception of Judaism they brought with them from Israel. The love that they have for him is heart-warming to see. They obviously trust and respect him immensely. Nechomie and the children are glowing, holy role models for these young people who were indoctrinated to distrust religious Jews.

While visiting this time, Rabbi Wilhelm told me the following story: On Shabbat, the crowd is too large (two hundred people!) to fit into the regular Chabad House, so they now use a hotel nearby for services and meals. One day, Rabbi Wilhelm received a call from a Satmar Chasid from the Williamsburg neighborhood of Brooklyn. He was in Thailand on business and wanted to know where he could stay for Shabbat. Rabbi Wilhelm suggested that he stay at that particular hotel so that he could attend the Shabbat services and share in the meals. He did so, and was greatly impressed by the whole experience. It was quite a revelation to him. That Friday night, he asked Rabbi Wilhelm, "How come all these young people come to you so happily? They would never come to me!"

The next morning, Shabbat day, he again approached Rabbi Wilhelm and said soberly, "You know, I couldn't sleep last night, thinking of what is happening here. I finally realized and came to the conclusion that the reason these people don't come to me is because I don't open my door to them!" Emotionally, he told Rabbi Wilhelm, "Rabbi, you should know that the biggest returnee to Torah observance you have made here is me!"

Changing The Rest Of The World

It would be a mistake to convey the impression that only the men and women specifically sent out by the Rebbe or his staff are emissaries. Anyone who reaches out to another Jew to inspire him or her to greater observance of the mitzvahs is an emissary. But let's go one further: anyone who reaches out to anyone – Jew or Gentile – is doing G-d's work. Let me tell you about Frances.

Frances Chang (not her real name) is a young woman who worked at the same office I once worked at in Manhattan. We had never been especially friendly with each other — no reason, except that we were both busy with our own duties. I had always tried to be pleasant with her so as to make a good impression as a Jew, but I had not sought her out to tell her about the Noahide Laws, the seven principles established by G-d for the non-Jewish nations to live by.

But one day, after returning from a trip to the Far East, the subject came up. When I first returned, my mind was still pre-occupied with the incredible amount of idol worship I had seen while there. It always shocks me anew to see people bending down, bowing to pieces of wood and stone, or making offerings of food, incense and flowers to these idols. I just can't help think about how wonderful it would be if their misplaced worship of these inanimate hunks of wood and stone could be redirected to the Creator of the Universe. How delighted He would be by their devotion.

And so I guess I said something about that one day to Frances. Maybe that was ill-advised in this politically correct, true-for-me, true-for-you world. But I did. I said how odd it seemed to see people putting food and drink in front of a stone idol, as though the stone could appreciate it! And Frances, who was a devout Buddhist, tried to explain it all to me. "We don't see the idols eating and drinking," she said, "because they do it spiritually. We must honor them." I, in turn, told her about how Abraham, when he was just three years old, came to know that there is but one G-d and that all the idols were false; how Abraham's father had been a dealer in idols, buying and selling them; and how one day when his mother and father were away, young Abraham took a big hammer and smashed all the idols except one, because they were an offense to the One G-d. When his parents returned, Abraham tried to explain to them that all the smaller idols had been smashed by the big one who remained. But his parents – buyers and sellers of idols though they were – didn't believe that! Even they knew, they said, that these were inert pieces of stone and wood that lacked the ability to do anything on their own.

We talked for a tong time, and I had a chance to tell Frances about the One G-d, the One who loved her very much. In speaking from the heart, I told her that she should devote her energies to G-d, not to the powerless pieces of stone and wood that the One G-d had created.

Nothing happened at once, of course, but little by little, I could tell that Frances had heard me. She seemed happier, and was more kind in her dealings with other people. She even dressed differently. Eventually she threw away her idols, saying that she recognizes them for the worthless objects they were.

This was a lesson for me. I had paid no real attention to Frances before, whereas now I know that there is no one who can't be reached by G-d's love and concern for them — and that includes "the nations," even those who describe themselves as devout Buddhists.

℘

After this, Frances was very open about asking questions about G-d, about Jewish life and practices, and about the things we believed and lived.

I could tell that one of the things that concerned her – troubled her, even – was the issue of charity. In Hebrew, the word we use is *tzedakah,* which doesn't actually mean charity at all. It means *justice.* So when we give *tzedakah* to someone less fortunate, someone in need, it isn't charity — a word that comes from the Latin *caratas,* which means something closer to love or compassion. We give to others because it is just to do so. Everything we have comes from G-d; every dollar that enters our hands, by whatever means, was placed there by G-d. And if that is the case, then it is only *just* for us to move some of that money along to others who have a need. In fact, a minimum of ten percent of our income, however much it may be, is simply not ours to spend on our own needs. At least ten percent must be given to others, in the name of G-d, because it really all belongs to Him to begin with. It's like He pays us ninety percent to do the work of distributing ten percent for Him.

But to Frances the Buddhist, this all seemed strange. She was there the day I told the new receptionist that no one who came to the door asking for money was to be turned away — they would all be given something, the amount depending on how much I had on hand. Frances bristled at this, I could tell. In her gentle and protective way, she was concerned about me. She knew how hard I worked for the money I earned. It galled her to see me giving it away to people I had never met, people who, she said, "probably don't deserve it."

Because of my hectic schedule, I occasionally order clothes and other things from catalogs. One day a jacket I had ordered was delivered to my home. Not only was it the wrong size, but once I saw the jacket, I realized I didn't like it at all. Bad choice. I was ready to rewrap it and sent it back, but then I thought, "What about Frances?" I knew that money was tight for her — her husband had deserted her, leaving her with a mountain of bills and debts, some of them supposedly for items she had never even seen. She was always short of money and, as I now remembered, her jacket was looking shabby.

Impulsively, I put the jacket back in the box and took it to work with me in the morning. As soon as Frances arrived, I gave it to her, asking her to try it on. After some serious begging she did … and it was perfect! The size and style were just right for her, and I could tell she loved it. But would she keep it when I told her it was a gift? No way, she insisted. She would pay me for it. I, in turn, insisted that it was a mitzvah for me to be able to give it to her. "Please," I said, "let me just do this. It will mean so much to me."

Finally, I explained the idea of Jewish *tzedakah*, justice. I was obligated, I told her, to pass ten percent along. After much discussion, she agreed to accept the jacket, but with tears in her eyes, she told me something I will never forget. "Now I understand," she said. "I used to resent all those people who came to the door — you *know* I did! I could not understand why you gave them your money, when they didn't deserve it. But now I see. You Jews are different from the rest of us. Better, in many ways. We keep our money to ourselves, but you share it with others. I have never given charity in my life, but now I will. If that is what your G-d wants, I will give!"

In the weeks and months that followed, Frances' references to *"your* G-d" evaporated. She may not be a full believer yet, but she told me many times that she now prays to the "One G-d" – now *her* G-d, I understand! – every night, asking Him to help her with her many problems. And she was comforted. As she put it: "Now I don't feel so alone. I know there is always Someone there to help me!"

And the *tzedakah* coin box in our office started filling up faster than it used to. I wondered why ...

The Hunger For Meaning

We should never underestimate the hunger of a Jewish soul for a way back to its Creator.

One of the most inspiring sights I've ever been privileged to see was a group of women suddenly and simultaneously grasping the idea of *mikvah* and – although it was new to virtually all of them – embracing it as a unit with excitement and enthusiasm.

It was a memorable night. I had been giving the first part of my two-part presentation on *mikvah* at the Chabad House in Tenafly, New Jersey. There were a lot of women and the level of excitement was high, but the evening had run very late and I was sure there were more than a few with baby-sitter problems who needed to leave. I had planned to come back the next week to do the instruction on the actual laws, but as it turned out there was a special event that evening, and we could not hold the meeting at Chabad House. Then I had a cross-country trip scheduled, so I rather regretfully informed the ladies that it would be a month before I could get back.

They were astonished. And not happy. I heard a buzz of conversation, and then one lady stood up. "There is no way we can wait a month!" she said. "Come to my home next week — we can have the class there instead." It sounded fine to me, so she gave out the address, and everyone agreed to come.

But you know how it goes: things come up; some people might be reluctant to seek out a private home at night. I was quite sure that the second week's gathering would be smaller than the first.

How wrong I was! As soon as I walked into the home – a really lovely mansion, actually – I could hear from the level of noise that a lot of women were present already. As it turned out, all the women from the previous week were there, plus several more — both the hostess and a couple of other women had brought their friends, and their friends' friends! It was a huge crowd, and I was absolutely delighted with the attention and interest they showed in the how-to of Family Purity and *mikvah* (the first night was for the why). As might be expected, I had to go over some of the basic material for the newcomers, but I couldn't find a single objection. The questions and answers lasted long into the evening and, as usual, there was a line of women who wanted to talk privately afterward.

There was one group of ladies who particularly impressed me. They were all friends, and came from two camps: a Reform synagogue and a close-by Conservative center. Almost apologetically they told me that they were, variously, Reform and Conservative Jews, but that they loved the ideas I had been talking about. Would it be all right for them, as non-Orthodox Jews, to perform this mitzvah, too?

"Of course," I said, hardly containing my delight even as I was surprised by the question. "This is for all Jews! There are no divisions here, no 'Reform,' 'Conservative,' and no 'Orthodox,' either. We are Jews. That's all it takes for a mitzvah to be yours, your inheritance."

I encouraged them not to pin labels so casually — labels are for shirts! Rather, they should just begin with this one mitzvah and continue to grow. These ladies were among my most serious students, and G-d bless them for their willingness to be open to something new, something that was, in actual fact, far outside of their previously-embraced culture. It was just wonderful to see the delight in their eyes.

There was one woman that night that who, among all the enthusiasm, caught my attention as I was speaking. I'm embarrassed to say it, but I caught myself looking at her from time to time because she was yawning so often. I started worrying whether I was boring, but as I watched, I could see that she was just very exhausted. After the class I went up to her and asked if she was all right. "Oh, I am," she said, "but my daughter was sick last night and I didn't get any sleep."

I told her I admired her spirit. If I had been in a similarly sleep-deprived condition, I wasn't sure I would have ventured out to a class. She suddenly sprang to life. "You mean miss this?" she asked. "How could I?! When would I ever have this opportunity again? This was so important!"

I am constantly impressed, delighted and humbled by the level of dedication of our Jewish women. Once they have seen a glimmer of light, they plunge right in to grasp it in its entirety. Did these women stop to ask, "How much do I have to do? Will this be difficult?" Not as far as I could tell. Once they got a taste of the blessings that come from one mitzvah, they wanted more, and more, and more.

The Bride To Be

Most Jews seem to know what a mezuzah is. A mezuzah is the small scroll of parchment on which is hand-printed two passages from the Torah. First, the Shema: "Hear O Israel, the L-rd our G-d, the L-rd is One" (*Deuteronomy* 6:4-9). And second: "And if you will carefully obey My mitzvahs ..." (*Deuteronomy* 11:13-21).

The Hebrew word mezuzah means doorpost, but it is used to refer to the parchment itself — not to the artistic and decorative holder most people admire. The purpose of a mezuzah is not to be a lucky charm or amulet, or to bring good luck into the house, although it does protect. It is instead a very serious mitzvah, not optional, one which we perform for no other reason than that we have been commanded to perform it.

It is extremely important that the requirements for the mitzvah of mezuzah be carefully adhered to. First, the mezuzah scroll must be kosher — a set of requirements too detailed to go into here, but basically the words must be hand-written (not photocopied or machine printed) on an actual piece of parchment (from a kosher animal, and not a piece of paper) without any errors or even imperfectly-formed letters. Second, the mezuzah must be correctly affixed to the doorpost, in a certain location, either at a slight slant as Ashkenazic (European) Jews do, or straight up, as is the Sephardic

(Middle Eastern) tradition. Finally, it is affixed to the door-post with a blessing.

In Chassidic philosophy, a properly produced and mounted mezuzah functions as a spiritual "helmet" of sorts, shielding one's life from mishaps and unfortunate events. Thus, when such things occurred, the Rebbe would often advise blessing-seekers to inspect their mezuzahs, rectifying situations by rectifying defective mezuzahs.

Now, it is easy to see how things can go wrong — it is quite common to discover a mezuzah that is not kosher. Either there is a problem with the writing or spelling, or the words have faded or the ink has run from exposure to moisture. Maybe it was never kosher in the first place. But as we have emphasized before, little things mean a lot in the performance of mitzvahs. That is most certainly true of the mitzvah of mezuzah.

One lady who found that out was Tzivia; a very attractive, accomplished and personable young woman of marriageable age who, for some reason, had never been able to find a suitable mate. She was my friend's niece and lived in London.

Several times a prospective, desirable suitor had been suggested, and each time there would be some problem, and the match fell through. No one could quite figure this out, since there was nothing wrong at all with Tzivia. She was lovely — although she was getting a little worried, needless to say.

The family was perplexed — they couldn't quite imagine

what the problem could be. They decided to ask the Rebbe for advice and a blessing. The Rebbe's answer was short and to the point: "Check your mezuzahs!"

Now the family was really puzzled. They bought their mezuzahs from a reputable source — just about the only way a nonprofessional can determine if a mezuzah is kosher or not. They remembered buying each and every one from an impeccable supplier, no funny business at all. "Well," they thought, "the Rebbe was mistaken on this one," and they ignored the advice. Besides, another very suitable, very promising, suitor was coming at the end of the week, and surely this next young man would work out — everything pointed to a successful match.

Alas, their bewilderment was to continue as this match fell through, too. Still puzzled, and now unsure, they decided to have the mezuzahs checked despite their confidence in them. What did they have to lose, after all?

Checking the mezuzahs, actually, is no small matter. Each one has to be taken down from the doorpost and taken to a reputable authority who will analyze each and every letter of each written parchment — although today computer scanning software had drastically sped up the inspection process.

Armed with his screwdriver, Tzivia's father set out to take the mezuzah off the front door, which he did. And guess what! The mezuzah itself turned out to be perfectly kosher, but *it had been installed upside down!* They still took all the mezuzahs down and had them checked by a certified Torah scribe, but all were fine except for this one problem, which they were very careful not to repeat in putting them back up.

Exactly one week later a perfect match was made, and Tzivia is now a very happily married lady.

The Male Was Late

One of the most prominent leaders of our Persian community in Queens, New York, once confided to me that although he was blessed with nine lovely granddaughters, he still yearned for his first grandson.

I took him to the Rebbe for Dollars, and he asked for advice and a blessing. The Rebbe responded, "Check your mezuzahs and tefillin." The man was startled because these were two mitzvahs he was very passionate about keeping perfectly.

"All the mezuzahs in my home are kosher! We had them all checked!" he told me.

"Did you do your office ones?"

"I don't know … I didn't realize I had to do those."

"Well, you're supposed to do those as well."

You guessed it: there was an error, which they immediately corrected. And on the first day of the next Rosh Hashanah, they were blessed with a beautiful grandson! Soon after, his other children also celebrated the births of their respective sons, one after the other.

A Matter Of Trust

Once when I was in Israel to be with my mother, who was scheduled for surgery, I heard there was going to be a large after-Shabbat party at Kfar Chabad (Chabad Village) on a particularly joyous occasion. Since I would be in the area anyway, I really wanted to go — so I stayed with my mother all day, and then caught a taxi after Shabbat to take me to Kfar Chabad near Jerusalem.

As we approached Kfar Chabad, the taxi driver was puzzled about all the activity so late at night. "What could be going on?" he asked. So I explained, and before long he told me a story of his own experience with the Rebbe.

This driver was an Israeli Jew who had his own rabbi and was not a follower of Chabad. But he also had a sister who had been very ill. A malignant tumor had been found in her brain, and the whole family was distraught. The driver had heard some things about the Lubavitcher Rebbe, and decided to try asking for his help and advice. He sent off a letter to the Rebbe, asking for help and a blessing, submitting his sister's name and their mother's name as well.

He received an immediate response from the Rebbe in New York: "Your sister should have her mezuzahs checked!"

The driver was a little surprised, and showed the letter to his own rabbi, who scoffed at it. "Listen," he told the driver. "The Lubavitcher Rebbe can't possibly answer all the mail he gets. This is probably his standard answer: 'Tell everyone who writes about an illness to get their mezuzahs checked!' Who's to know otherwise? It's good advice, anyway."

There was, of course, no truth to what the rabbi said. The Rebbe always read his mail.

But the driver thought there might be something to it — and besides, what could it hurt? He decided to trust the Rebbe and have all of his sister's mezuzahs checked, plus her husband's tefillin. To their surprise, almost all of them were not kosher — they either had been poorly made years ago or had suffered weather damage, which meant that the words could not even be read. They immediately replaced all the damaged parchments with new, kosher ones, and then waited for the miracle.

At the next doctor's appointment, everyone was astonished to learn that the tumor had shrunk considerably. They decided to wait before going ahead with the scheduled – and very dangerous – surgery, and sure enough, little by little, the tumor kept shrinking until it was completely gone. Even in telling me the story, the taxi driver couldn't help crying — and he did not weep alone. It was an inspiring story, one so full of trust and hope and faith that it bears retelling, over and over.

In keeping the mitzvahs, little things mean a lot!

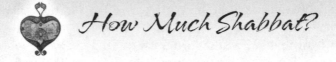

How Much Shabbat?

One of the men in our community was having terrible financial problems. Although he worked very hard at his business, success eluded him, year after year. Every deal that came up looked like a sure winner – the one that would at last put him on a firm financial footing – before it crashed with a thud, leaving him in a more precarious position than he had been before. He had every disaster you can imagine: major customers didn't pay him, employees stole his merchandise, a bookkeeper embezzled, his suppliers cancelled desirable contracts — you name it. He was like a modern-day, businessman version of Job.

As you might expect, all this bad luck also caused him to become very depressed. The time came when he hardly dared take any action. With all the problems he'd been through, he couldn't help but wonder what disaster would fall on his head with *this* one. If a deal looked good and he jumped in, he would lose his shirt. If a deal looked especially good, he would be suspicious and pass it up — and someone else would make millions. What to do now?

One day, when everything seemed to have hit absolute rock bottom, he stopped by to visit my husband, and we got to talking. He was so forlorn, I could hardly believe this was the vigorous, vibrant man I had known a couple of years ago. He was emotionally on his last legs.

I mentioned how many people had received some very good advice from the Rebbe. Why didn't he ask the Rebbe for help? At least for a blessing?

I could see he was interested, but I could also see he would never do it. Once a person feels so beaten down that he loses hope, even doing a simple thing like standing in line for Dollars seems like another pointless mountain to climb. So I told him I would, with his permission, write a letter to the Rebbe on his behalf. I would tell what I knew of his problems, and ask for a blessing for financial success.

I wrote the letter and gave it in to the Rebbe's office. The answer back was almost immediately. The Rebbe gave him his blessing, but added, "Do not work on Shabbat or holidays!" We were stunned, all of us. These were observant Jews, so far as we knew. I had no idea he would work on the Shabbat, or on special festival days. Neither, as it turned out, had his wife known. But he did — he would just disappear from everyone's radar screen for several hours on Saturday afternoons, from time to time, and everyone assumed he was resting, reading, or somewhere else. But he was now ready to admit it: He had been so worried about his business that he had, in fact, been putting in "just a few hours of work" on the Shabbat.

He was embarrassed, of course, but more than that, he was astonished. How in the world had the Rebbe known? His *wife* didn't know! His family had no idea! No one in the community had even the slightest idea! But the Rebbe knew. It was an astounding revelation.

— On Mitzvahs —

It was so astounding that he stopped to think: If the Rebbe knew, then obviously he wasn't fooling G-d, either — not that he thought he was, of course. He'd just been so worried ...

But these things do matter to G-d, and a "few hours" of work on the Shabbat, the Jewish day of rest, are very important. *Very* important. And if it mattered so much to G-d, of course he would stop doing it.

Today, this man is still not a millionaire, but he and his family are happy, he is earning a very good living, and best of all, he now doesn't have to spend any of it on psychiatrists and medications. His life has taken on new meaning — all by completely following that one little law about not working, *at all,* on the Shabbat!

"What? What Did You Say?"

A few years ago I was asked to take a family to the Rebbe for a blessing. Joseph, a very successful Iranian businessman, was in a state of hysteria because he had just learned that his beloved mother had been diagnosed with cancer. It was decided that all three would go to Dollars: the sick mother, Joseph and his wife.

We went as a group, and I witnessed the following scene: Joseph asked for a blessing from the Rebbe, saying, "My mother here is sick." The Rebbe's answer was immediate: "Give more *tzedakah.*" But Joseph thought the Rebbe hadn't heard him, so he repeated, a little louder, "No, I said my mother is sick!" The Rebbe again said, "Give more *tzedakah.*" Joseph was still confused. "NO," he began again, "you don't understand. MY MOTHER. SICK." The Rebbe just smiled, and Rabbi Groner, the Rebbe's assistant, put his hand on Joseph's arm, telling him that the Rebbe knew his mother was sick. "The Rebbe is suggesting giving more money to charity to make your mother better."

When Joseph understood that, he was delighted. "Is that all? I can do that!" And he did — he gave considerable amounts to several different funds, all with joy and delight, now fully confident that if he followed the Rebbe's directive, his mother would be restored to health.

And in no time at all, she was.

On Inspiration

Prayer Equals Instant Gratification... Right?

In today's world, we are used to instant gratification and easily become frustrated with anything that can't be accomplished immediately. With our cell phones, we can contact almost anyone, instantly, complaining if we get an answering machine instead. On our computers, we can connect to any Web site around the world, even as we complain that it takes five whole seconds to load! In jet airplanes we fly across the continent in less time than it took our ancestors to hitch up the wagons and ride to the nearest town, yet we complain about the food the airlines serve. We have accustomed ourselves to having whatever we want: food, communication, travel, health, wealth and education, and all right now, without delay.

Life isn't always that compliant. And neither is G-d.

It's true, of course, that some prayers are answered instantly. Remember the story of Eliezer going to seek out a bride for Isaac? As he approached a public well, he prayed that somehow the right woman would be shown to him. Before he even finished his prayer, a lovely young woman named Rebecca came up and asked if she could fetch water for him and his camels. He knew he had found the right girl!

But Eliezer was especially virtuous (which can't hurt when asking favors of G-d). Most of the time, the truth is, we don't get instant results — unless that was what G-d intended in the first place. More frustrating yet is the fact that while all prayers are answered, not all are answered with "yes." Even in some of the examples we've seen, G-d has answered the prayers, but in the way He knew was best for us all along.

The life story of my precious daughter-in-law is especially illustrative. Her name was Yocheved.

Yocheved's Story

Even as a teenager, Yocheved seemed special, perhaps gifted. One especially appealing quality was her extra dose of spiritual beauty, which shone most brightly in her acts of charity. There are so many examples, but one will have to do. One time, Yocheved's high school class was directed to write a story about "The Most Special Jewish Woman I Know." She wrote about a delightful, handicapped, wheelchair-bound Jewish woman named Rose whom she visited and helped every week in her poor apartment in the most dangerous part of the Bronx. The essay was so outstanding that the teacher submitted it to a competition, where it won the $500 first prize. What did Yocheved do with the award? She gave it to Rose, of course.

Yocheved was just sixteen when a spark of yearning began to stir deep inside. Her creative and probing mind sought what was important and meaningful in life. On her own she asked, read, questioned and sought until she concluded a fully observant Orthodox Jewish life was her destiny. Despite the challenges of living in a nonreligious community and the real possibility of losing her friends, she proudly marched to the beat of her own inner drum with great determination.

Shortly after beginning her personal journey, she was introduced by our rabbi to my son, David Yecheskel. He suggested the match because he felt it would be a good one, and they were the only two observant teens that age in the area. They only met once, but it was enough for them to know that they were destined for each other. David was home from seminary at the time and shortly returning to Israel for six more months of study. Although they were both just seventeen at the time, they made known their intention to get married when he returned.

I already loved Yocheved, but I was overwhelmed with confusion. Probably ninety percent of everyone and anyone we knew opposed the marriage. "They're so young," I kept hearing. I needed an unbiased opinion. I needed special advice.

The Rebbe, the leader of the Chabad Lubavitch Chassidim, is generally understood to be an exceptionally righteous person whose personal perfection produces an awareness that transcends the apparent boundaries of existence. Hundreds of letters and faxes would arrive daily for the Rebbe, seeking his wise and sagely insight into life's complex and challenging trials and concerns.

I poured my heart out on paper and mailed a letter. The Rebbe's answer was surprising in its lack of equivocation. "They *should* get married," he wrote, "and they should move to Israel." And he added, "Anyone who tries to stop this [match] should take it on their own responsibility!" Intuitively I knew it all along, but I needed someone I trusted in my corner. It was decided: I would help them. With my permission and help, the couple planned to be married secretly. For weeks I shopped for a dress and household items, but the flurry of activity could hardly be kept secret. Little by little the word got out. The rest of the family came around and consented on the condition that they not move to Israel and that David first get a job for six months. Reluctantly, David and Yocheved agreed. At least they could be married out in the open.

The wedding was a powerful experience and inspirational to all. Many in our family and community were delighted and stirred to see the beautiful, familiar rituals. Yocheved's joy made a deep impression on many people — could it be that this young girl sensed something about the beauty of living a Jewish life that *they*, so much older and wiser, had somehow missed?

They were our frequent Shabbat guests. Yocheved would light the Shabbat candles and sometimes remain standing in place for over an hour, singing and praying. I'd usually slip out of the room — somehow it felt as though I was intruding on her intense dialogue with G-d.

G-d places tests and obstacles in our path so that we overcome them and thereby bring to the fore our inner, latent strengths and talents. He had His tests for Yocheved. The first was becoming observant. The second was to marry her soulmate despite the opposition. The third was to prove much more difficult. Although the couple expected to start a family right away, months and months passed without a pregnancy.

It certainly was not for lack of petition. Yocheved seemed to storm the heavens with her fervent prayers. "G-d must certainly give in pretty soon," I remember thinking. "How could He possibly say no to such a heartrending appeal?" Her persistence was staggering, and after two long years the couple was blessed with a beautiful baby girl, Yael Sarah.

But the final test was yet to come. Two years after Yael's birth, Yocheved was diagnosed with cancer of the liver. The doctors looked solemn — it had already spread to her lungs and abdomen. "Two to three months to live," I heard them say. Yocheved refused to accept a no hope, no cure judgment. "You're not G-d! No one but G-d can tell me when I will die!" she countered, and took action accordingly.

Everyone pitched in — I cooked macrobiotic food, we took her to every kind of specialist, and my son took her to Israel to pray at the Western Wall and to visit holy men for advice. She felt wonderful while in Israel.

Yocheved followed the ancient Jewish custom of adding a second name to garner additional spiritual strength, choosing Ruchamah, or "merciful." And the prayers came pouring in from everywhere. People who hadn't prayed in years and were moved by the story started saying prayers and reading Psalms — many of them complete strangers. As news of her illness spread, letters arrived from around the world. Many people, old and young, resolved to start doing mitzvahs in her merit. In her former school, a four hour "Gossip-Free Period" was established when no detrimental speech about others was permitted. A young man who hadn't put on tefillin since his bar mitzvah six years before told me, "I wanted to pray for Ruchamah Yocheved, but how could I do that when I wasn't even putting on tefillin? Now I pray with tefillin every weekday morning, and ask G-d to let her live!" We received a call from the dean of a religious school in Israel, who said that extra learning was being done for Yocheved's benefit. On Purim, a group of our friends went to my daughter-in-law in the hospital. A joyous celebration erupted, complete with singing. The entire hospital floor joined our happy celebration and delicious meal.

By now, Yocheved was on chemotherapy and becoming thin and weak, but her dazzling smile and warm welcome never faded. She actually comforted the people who came to visit.

I remember one day, after an excruciatingly painful procedure, Yocheved was wheeled back to her room in such pain she could hardly breathe. She whispered for me to find her "special" little prayer book, together with the list of needy people she was praying for every day. She never missed a day of prayers and was always asking for more names. One day she saw that the Jewish lady next to her in the hospital was receiving visits from a clergyman representing a religion that was foreign to Judaism. "Why are you doing this?" Yocheved pleaded, begging her not to see him anymore. "What is the difference?" responded the unfortunate lady. "If you promise me you will never see him again, I will give you something very special," Yocheved answered. "My lucky prayer book." And she listened.

On Yom Kippur 1993, almost a full year after she had been given two to three months to live, Yocheved fasted all night and day. In a superhuman display of courage, she prayed the entire service standing up without taking any of the painkillers that kept her functioning. I was there; I saw it all. It was in my home.

One week later, on Simchat Torah, our beloved Yocheved slipped peacefully into a coma. To the very end she believed that she would be saved. My son was at her side. The doctor told him to prepare for the end, which could come any minute — the cancer had reached her heart. But for two weeks our Yocheved fought on, not wanting to leave her husband and daughter. We kept a vigil by her bedside, talking to her, praying, even eating and sleeping there, never leaving her alone. One day, her eyes fluttered and her lips moved. Her parents, husband, teacher, rabbi, Benjamin and I were all there. A half-hour later, in perfect peace, she returned her pure soul to her Maker.

Yocheved's life may have been short in its twenty-four years, but it was filled with good deeds and inspiration. Her doctor, who had been a totally nonobservant Jew, came to understand that it had been Yocheved's soul that kept her body functioning. He was constantly filled with wonderment. Many others who had been distant in their relationship to G-d, now began to keep mitzvahs. So many people told me how inspired they were by Yocheved's complete and uncompromising love for G-d despite her trials. "Always appreciate what you have," she was fond of saying. She asked me to share it as her message.

ℒ

But she was only physically gone. Soon after her passing, she appeared in a dream to my youngest daughter, Daniella Miriam, who enjoyed an especially close bond with Yocheved.

"You must come and see my new apartment!" Yocheved said to Daniella.

"But Yocheved, you can't stay there! We are waiting for you down here!"

"You just can't understand why it has to be this way," Yocheved smiled gently. "To me, it is so clear now."

That was Yocheved. Always deeply concerned for others' feelings, even reaching out from Heaven to console her loved ones and assuage their sense of loss.

Perhaps the greatest miracle is little Yael Sarah, who celebrated her fourth birthday the week before her mother passed. As we lit the candles that Shabbat night, she called out all on her own, "Please, G-d, please send Moshiach now, so my Mommy can come down and I can hug and kiss her!"

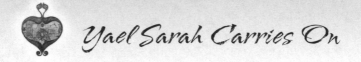

Yael Sarah Carries On

Rabbi Lazer Naness, of blessed memory, a venerable senior Lubavitcher Chasid who lived in Israel, played a very important part in my life and that of my family. When my son David was studying in Israel, he spent much gainful time learning with Rabbi Naness. And every time I went to Israel, I would always find time to go see him, asking for his kind blessing and his brilliant and loving advice.

There was only one time that Rabbi Naness ever wavered from his usual gentle, sweet smile and kindly, patient answers to my many questions. That was when Ruchamah Yocheved was so very ill and I asked him to please pray for a full recovery for her. That time, to my surprise, he seemed to sink back in his chair and, after a long silence, he said that he was very sorry, but he was so tired, so exhausted, so ill himself, that he could not do that for me. He suggested I ask the Rebbe instead — which of course I already had. Shortly thereafter, Ruchamah Yocheved passed away.

It was about two years later that I was back in Israel and again went to visit Rabbi Naness, to tell him all that had happened. I also told him that my son David and granddaughter Yael Sarah were very lonely, and that they needed a wife and mother (not that my son said so at that time). This time, the rabbi smiled and responded quickly, saying, "Your son will be married again soon and happier than before!"

Several months after Ruchamah Yocheved left us, a next-door neighbor of David's, a young man named Adam who happened to be the son of a longtime friend of our family, approached my son. "My wife has a very good match for you!" he informed him, explaining that the girl he was referring to had been a schoolmate of his wife. "They were in seminary together in Montreal," he said. "She was married for a few months and then suffered a divorce through no fault of her own. She's wonderful — can we arrange a meeting?"

At this time David was still several months short of his twenty-sixth birthday, and was far from recovered from the loss of Yocheved. He was still saying Kaddish, the special eleven-month praise of G-d in merit of the dead. How could he even think of another match? It was too early, he thought. He politely said no; thank you, but no.

Two years passed. We were all still mourning the loss of Yocheved, but my son was inconsolable. If it hadn't been for his precious little daughter, who was wise beyond her years, I don't know what would have become of him. Yael Sarah was four years old when her mother died, and now another two years had passed. It was she, and she alone, who could tell her father what he needed to hear.

One night, Yael Sarah had an ear infection and was staying at our home. David was sitting at her bedside and reading her a story.

Suddenly she said, "Daddy, until Moshiach comes and brings down Mommy from Heaven, please bring me a *new* Mommy! Then when Moshiach comes, I will have *two* mommies!" We were all stunned. Yael Sarah went on. "I mean it, Daddy! I want brothers and sisters — please bring me a new Mommy!"

She was serious. She simply wouldn't give her father any rest. She'd ask him in the morning, at night and any other time she thought about it, which was often. When he came home from work she would ask, "Well, Daddy, did you find me a Mommy today?" And if he would just say "No," she would patiently explain to him how it should be done: "Look harder, Daddy — you can't wait for her to come to *you!* Please try harder, ask more people to help!"

Well, if G-d can respond to impassioned and incessant requests, so could my son. How could he possibly refuse his little angel's wistful request for something every little girl deserves — a mommy and siblings? So he agreed: If any suitable introductions were set up for him, he would go out.

There was a small problem, however. By now he was twenty-six, and all the girls that were proposed for him were too young — in our community, young women marry at about twenty. So, although many suitable matches were proposed, he didn't believe that any of them were capable of being a good Mommy to his precocious little six-year-old.

It seems, though, that Adam and his wife never gave up on their idea, and Adam approached David again. "Remember that classmate of my wife's I told you about? Well, she is now prepared to consider marriage. What about you? Can we arrange a meeting now?" After consulting with his rabbi, David agreed.

And this time, the timing was perfect — my son flew to Montreal to meet Chana Devorah, a fine girl from a wonderful family. They both realized that they were indeed intended for each other. After just one meeting, they decided to marry, but decided to meet one more time.

Up to now, David had kept little Yael Sarah out of the proceedings, to avoid any disappointment that might result. But now, she had to be told. She had wanted a mommy, but what would she think if she saw a potential one in person? An idealized mommy might be fine. But how would she deal with a real one?

Our worries were unfounded. As soon as Yael Sarah set eyes on Chana Devorah from across the room, she ran to her, calling to her, "Mommy, Mommy!" Once again, everyone was stunned, but she went on, "I *know* she's my new Mommy — I saw her in my dreams!" To everyone's amazement, she went on to describe, in considerable detail, exactly what Chana Devorah's hair covering and other things looked like. And, no, she had never actually seen any of them.

From that day on, Yael Sarah was one happy little girl — but no happier than my son, or any of the other members of the family. To add to the blessing, everyone had an instant baby sister — little Deena, and exactly one year later, another little sister, Avigayil, to be joined in due time by Shlomo, Yosef, Batsheva and Yutta Brocha. Rabbi Naness had been right.

Chassidic philosophy teaches us that our prayers should be as pure as a child's. This little child, Yael Sarah, was tested by G-d at a very early age, and still was able to pray to her Father in Heaven for what she wanted: a Mommy. She received exactly what she wanted.

One night, not too long ago, I was baby-sitting and Yael Sarah and I were having a conversation. "I know that before, everyone thought I was sleeping when I would go to bed," she said shyly. "But, you know, I was not. I would just lie there, talking to G-d, asking Him to send me a new Mommy. And you know? He really understands and listens!"

Out of the mouth of a very knowledgeable little girl!

"Here. Take It With My Blessing."

Before we get caught up with the idea that G-d *does* answer prayer, but perhaps not as quickly as we would like, or not exactly the way we would like, let's take a look at a few situations in which results were not only clear and convincing but also instantaneous. It wasn't only Eliezer, servant of Abraham, who got G-d's attention right away!

I know I'm chronologically confusing you here, but allow me to take you back to the early days of my involvement with the Lubavitcher Rebbe, which lands us in the early '80s. The Rebbe started Dollars in 1985, and before that, there was a custom for people to stand along his path when he went from his office to the synagogue for the daily afternoon prayer. Just having the privilege to see his smile, maybe hear a word or two, was well worth the trip — as we will see.

One day in 1981 I took two ladies with me. They were strangers to each other, but both were Iranian, so I had hoped they'd get along well. On the way, in my car, one of them began to complain bitterly about her rheumatism, which was bothering her a great deal. She really went on and on — more than your standard *kvetching*. The other lady was silent, and at some point, the complainer turned to the silent one and said, "And I suppose you are in perfect health!"

The silent one said, quietly, "No. I have cancer."

Silence. And a good lesson to remember, in the I-complained-because-I-had-no-shoes-until-I-met-a-man-who-had-no-feet tradition.

In any event, the lady with the cancer had just had a mastectomy, which in the early '80s also included the removal of a great deal of muscle and tissue from under the arm, in a wide arc around the chest area. As a result of the removal of the muscle and nerve tissue, she no longer had any feeling at all in her arm or hand. Neither could she control that limb, but rather used the other arm to keep it pressed tightly to her side. We reached 770, got out of the car, and found a place to stand along the already-crowded walkway. Right on time, the Rebbe walked past, went into the synagogue and prayed the afternoon service. We decided to wait for his return journey, and in just a short while, he emerged.

This time he was walking more leisurely, and as he passed us, he immediately stopped and turned back. He looked directly at the lady with cancer and gave her a broad smile. Reaching into his pocket, he pulled out a coin and held it out to her. In his position, he was very near her lifeless hand and arm.

She instinctively reached out for whatever he was offering ...with that "useless" arm. She burst into tears, sobbing out her gratitude.

And the Rebbe completed his walk, smiling that knowing, gentle smile of his.

The lady later reported that a warm glow traveled up her hand and arm. Full feeling and motion were instantly restored as she took the coin. As we drove home, she kept exclaiming, "My arm! I can feel my arm! And it doesn't hurt!" Over and over. From that moment on, she was able to use her hand and arm normally, as before the surgery.

This remarkable lady – Chaya Margalit was her name – was not a complainer. It was not only during that ride to 770 that she didn't complain. She *never* did. Not about anything. And if you knew more about her life and her struggles, you would agree that if she had wanted to, she would have had the right to a whole lot more complaining than any of us. But she was always happy and confident that everything, whatever it was, was for the best. Bless her for her complete and simple faith — something the Rebbe must have seen when he reached out to her with that coin and that smile.

Instant Gratification

My parents had a story of their own about instantaneous help from G-d.

My paternal grandparents are interred on the Mount of Olives, in Jerusalem. Unfortunately, during the years of 1948 to 1967, the Jordanians were in control of that area and they used the holiest Jewish cemetery in unthinkable ways — latrines were built with gravestones, hovels for people to live in were erected right on the grave sites and the site was desecrated in many more ways with actions too painful to recount.

After the 1967 Six Day War, when the land was so miraculously liberated and put back in its rightful Jewish hands, my parents, who were living in London at that time, decided to make the trip to Israel to see if they could find the burial sites of my father's parents. After all my parents' generation had endured, being able to visit the graves and pay the proper respects at their parents' gravestones would mean a great deal to them, and was well worth the travel.

Baba and Mummy (remember, I'm British!) flew to Israel, recovered from the stress of travel, and summoned a taxi to take them to the Mount of Olives. The only information they had as to where the graves actually were in that huge cemetery was that they were "near Yad Avshalom," the grave marker of King David's son Avshalom. Not very helpful, what with no markers or maps or anything else at that time right after the war. Nonetheless, they were determined to go.

The taxi arrived. Baba and Mummy told the driver they wanted to go to the cemetery. He was incredulous: "You can't be serious! You think you can find two graves among the tens of thousands that are there?" But then he warmed to the subject and started to explain. "Don't you know the Arabs ripped up all the gravestones? They carted them off and built toilets! Ramshackle houses were built on that land — everything was leveled. Don't you understand? You'll never find any specific grave there. It's just not possible." To give him his due, he was speaking against his own interest. "Save your money," he kept saying. "Don't even try. It's hopeless."

But Baba and Mummy had come all this way and they were determined not to be talked out of it now. "It is our duty to observe the mitzvah to honor our parents, and we must at least try. It is important that we at least make a good effort!" So they got into the cab and drove off.

Now, this was in the Israeli summer. To those of you who know, I needn't describe the heat. To those of you who haven't experienced an Israeli summer yet, I can only say that it can be quite literally life-threatening to be out under the sun for very long, especially at midday, which it now was. As the cab pulled up at a random spot a short distance from one of the entrances to the cemetery and stopped, my father asked him to please wait. They couldn't be gone very long — it was far too hot. The driver shrugged, and agreed. He settled back for a rest, and assumed it would be only a few minutes before they would give up and scurry for the relative cool of the cab.

My parents walked the short distance to what remained of what must have been a part of the old cemetery gate and went through. They, too, knew they wouldn't be able to remain outside long. Nevertheless, Baba and Mummy each took one side of the path, and started to look at the inscriptions.

And there they were!

Right in front of my father stood the double headstones that marked the graves of my father's parents! Baba and Mummy began to shout in joy, incredulous themselves at having immediately located the graves in this mess of rubble, weedy growth and debris. The taxi driver heard their cries and rushed to help, thinking they had fallen. When they pointed out the very graves they had been seeking, he, too, was thunderstruck — and, for once, speechless!

It was an open miracle. Not only that the gravestones had remained untouched and unvandalized, but also that they had found them so quickly, a task that was considered not just unlikely but outright impossible. After some time spent cleaning the headstones, and many tears of love and gratitude, they said some prayers, paid their respects, climbed back into the taxi and returned to their hotel.

The cab driver refused to accept a fare from them. He said he had just witnessed a miracle and had no intention of sullying it by taking a shekel for his participation.

And what's really a gift is how G-d accommodated my father, whom He knew very well: My father was infamous for not having much patience. If he had had to spend any more than a few minutes, he would have been the first to say, "That's it. Let's go."

Many years ago, G-d had those two particular graves of His faithful servants put just there. Then He protected them through years of Jordanian destruction and desecration. And then, after a miraculous war, He had my parents' cab driver drive right to that spot near it, and park there — and all so that a Jewish son could honor his deceased parents in the traditional way. How could anyone not love a G-d like that?

Heaven On The Holy Land

One year, ten days before Passover, I had to make an emergency trip to Israel. My mother had had a heart attack, and both she and my father needed some help. There are six of us brothers and sisters, but none of us lived in Israel at the time. Between us all, I was the most able to go. (As is my custom, I had gotten ready for Passover a full week early — something of a miracle in itself.)

On the El Al flight to Israel, I was fascinated by a large group of tourists going to Israel for the first time: a contingent of African-American Baptists from a church in Georgia. They were in extraordinarily high spirits at being able to visit "the Holy Land" — a very sacred place for their religion, too. I was sitting near a very large, dignified and proper man, a member of this party who eventually overcame his reticence and asked me to recommend some of the sites in Israel they should not miss.

"There's too much on our schedule," he said. "We won't be able to do it all. Which are the essential ones?"

I recommended a few, but had to add that he, as a Baptist, was able to go to historical sites that were not open to me as a Jew. At that time, I would not have been able to go to the graves of Abraham, Sarah and the rest of the Patriarchs and

Matriarchs in Hebron. Yet he, as a non-Jew, could get there. Those graves were within heavily guarded Arab territory – still are, actually – and the only way a Jew could have gone would have been to hire a private guard. A Jew in that place would have made an easy target for Arab sharpshooters. It was the same with Rachel's Tomb and other sacred Jewish sites — it was simply too dangerous, and hence not permitted, for a Jew to enter those areas alone.

My seatmate was astonished. He had never heard of such a thing. We began talking about the media coverage of the situation in Israel, and I was able to open his eyes on several matters. He had not heard, for example, that the "settlements" were on Jewish land. His assumption was that they were hostile incursions on Arab territory! And why wouldn't he think so? That is the message the media convey. He shook his head in wonder at my "revelations." He said they, as Baptists, believe in the Bible and acknowledge, as he said, that "you Jews are G-d's chosen people, His firstborn! We have to give you respect!"

Later, I heard him explaining all his new knowledge to his fellow travelers. It was nice to hear the truth getting out, even in such a small way. Now, if we could just convince the Israeli government of the truth!

ℒ

I spent several days with Baba and Mummy, helping them prepare for the great festival of our liberation from Egypt — and whichever Egypts we are slaves to in today's world. Then I decided one day to take a trip to the Western Wall.

I took a bus, carrying only my book of Psalms, which I started reading on the bus. I couldn't help but overhear some ladies behind me talking, however, and heard one of them identify herself as Chabad. Today, she was saying, was a very special day. My ears perked up at that — *what* was going on that I didn't know about? I finally had to turn to them to ask, and admit to them that I'd overheard their conversation.

They told me that today was the day that Joseph Gutnick, the Australian philanthropist, had arranged for a massive bar mitzvah for some of the Children of Chernobyl.

Children of Chernobyl is a Chabad-sponsored project to rescue as many Russian Jewish children as possible from the Chernobyl area that had been so victimized by the nuclear disaster. Chabad has worked for years to airlift them to Israel and tend to their needs for housing, food and, most of all, the advanced medical care only available in Israel.

On this particular day, Gutnick had funded dozens of these twelve-year-old Russian Jewish girls and thirteen-year-old Russian Jewish boys to come to Israel, to the Western Wall, for a communal bat/bar mitzvah. All were dressed in matching blouses (the girls) and white shirts (the boys), with neatly pressed black skirts and pants. All were given copies of the Torah, prayer books, tefillin and other Jewish gifts. And all had been studying and were now ready to assume their status as fully knowledgeable adult members of the worldwide

Jewish community. For most of them, this was the biggest milestone of their lives.

You can't imagine the joy — Jewish music of a kind that almost made the very stones get up and dance! Delicious food was overflowing. And, most of all, there were the dozens and dozens of these wonderful children who had gone through so very much, and still persevered, even at their tender ages. Behind them in the square were their parents and proud relatives, and then thousands upon thousands of well-wishers from the world over who had come to participate.

On a series of platforms in front was every Jewish dignitary you could think of — not only Chabad rabbis and teachers from all over the world, but also the Chief Rabbis of Israel, past and present, both Ashkenazic and Sephardic. The mayor of Jerusalem and political leaders of the Knesset were also on hand. The whole plaza was filled with flags, flowers, and pennants —a scene of beautiful colors, joy and celebration almost beyond comprehension.

And overlooking it all, as though he was there in person, was a huge picture of our smiling Rebbe (several stories tall!), looking down with that special love he had for all these children, of every age, assembled before the most holy site in Judaism, the only remnant we have of our once glorious Temple.

I couldn't stop crying — it was a taste, just a taste, of what it will be like when our long-awaited Moshiach comes, when the entire world will be filled with just such love and joy and peace in our dedication to our G-d.

The sun shone brightly that day, after a week of drizzle and rain, as though G-d Himself wanted to direct His warmth and blessing on everyone who had traveled so far, and with such dedication. The whole thing was miraculous: those children, rescued from a land of centuries of hatred crowned with science-gone-wrong destruction, had survived it all; Joseph Gutnick and his successes, that enabled Chabad to do this particular mitzvah; the glorious sun that appeared out of nowhere to bless us all with the warmth and light of G-d's never-ending love; and the Rebbe, who was not there physically, but whose spirit pervaded it all. It was his wisdom, his dedication, his foresight, and his plan to bring these children to this day of Jewish adulthood, there, in the Land of Israel, at the Western Wall.

The day, the crowds, the love, the warmth, the flowers and the music … they are all woven together in a sensory tapestry I can call up in my mind in its entirety any moment I wish. It will remain with me as long as I live.

Heaven on Earth. It was close.